Desert
Sojourn

A Woman's Forty Days and Nights Alone

D0391766

Debi Holmes-Binney

Seal Press

Cover design by Clare Conrad
Cover photograph by C. Angarola / The Image Bank
Text design by Alison Rogalsky

Library of Congress Cataloging-in-Publication Data
Holmes-Binney, Debi.
     Desert sojourn : a woman's forty days and nights alone / Debi Holmes-Binney.
         p. cm.
     Includes bibliographical references.
     ISBN 1-58005-040-9 (pbk.)
     1. Holmes-Binney, Debi—Journeys—Utah—Great Salt Lake Desert.
2. Great Salt Lake Desert (Utah)—Biography. I. Title.

CT275.H645518 A3 2000
917.92'430433'092—dc21   00-024093

Printed in the United States of America

Fonts: Papyrus, AGaramond and Type Embellishments

First printing, June 2000

10   9   8   7   6   5   4   3   2

Distributed to the trade by Publishers Group West
In Canada: Publishers Group West Canada, Toronto, Ontario

To Jerry

Author's Note

This book is based upon my true-life, forty-day retreat in the Great Salt Lake Desert, although the names of certain individuals and some other details have been changed for privacy and clarity.

Desert
Sojourn

Chapter One

Day 1, November 11

I wake to pitch black with no idea where I am. The terrifying thing is that I could be anywhere. For the past three years I've traveled almost constantly from coast to coast, north to south, back and forth. My mind struggles to make any sense of my surroundings. I'm in a bed, but it's not my own. I have no bed of my own. No bedroom, no kitchen, no home of my own, not anymore, but I am in a room.

My eyes dart around for anything familiar, even a clock. I rise to my elbows and notice the faint beam of a streetlight shining through a crack where rubber-lined curtains don't quite close. The beam strikes a television mounted on brackets high on the opposite wall. I don't see any glowing numbers on a digital clock, and the clues begin to come together. Motel 6s have rubber-lined curtains and HBO on channel 3, but they don't have clock radios. In a sudden gush I remember everything.

Motel 6. I checked in last night after driving all day, fourteen hours. Yesterday morning I watched seagulls float over the Pacific shore in California. Today I wake to a different shore. I am in Salt Lake City on the edge of the Great Salt Lake, on the edge of the Great Salt Lake Desert, one of the most remote and rugged wildernesses in the United States. The desert. That's why I've come.

The advantage of Motel 6s is that they're all almost exactly the same, and I've stayed in enough of them to locate the light over the faux wood bedstand even in the dark. I squint in the sudden glare to read the dial on my wind-up travel alarm. It never has glowed in the dark. 3:30 a.m. It was set to go off in fifteen minutes anyway.

The fog that first engulfed my mind is gone, and I take in the room's contents in a single sweeping glance—from the orange short-pile carpet to the mismatched blue-and-gold upholstered chairs, from the dresser that doubles as a coffee table to the floor-length mirror with a large gash in its pressboard frame. I slide one leg to the floor and then the other, slowly, deliberately, more deliberately than I have ever risen from bed before, aware as the sheets fold back that by tonight I will be in a place where there are no sheets at all. No bedstands, no lamps.

Flicking on the television to the local news, I pad across the room to a metal unit beneath the window that blows cold air in summer and hot in winter. I turn it full blast to the red zone. By tonight I'll be where there are no heaters. By tonight I'll be where there is no news.

The bathroom tile slickens with steam as hot water floods through the shower pipes. Stepping into the stall, I'm met with a meager but needle-sharp spray, making me all the more aware that by tonight I'll be in a place where there are no pipes, no hot water, no water at all. I dry myself with a towel hardly bigger than a pillow case, too small to reach across my back even if it wasn't frayed, but I'm more mindful of the fact that this is the last towel I will use, my last shower for forty days.

There will be no call for cosmetics where I'm going. Perhaps that's why I take extra care smoothing the foundation over my cheeks, scrutinizing my face as always for any possible flaw. I see hair that never does what I want it to do and eyebrows that need to be plucked. Stroking blush across my cheeks, I realize that I might as well be polishing my shoes, covering the blemishes for the sake of a public kind enough to overlook the scuffs and scrapes disguised by the polish. I only wish there was a makeup that could conceal the eyes' secret regrets. Perhaps that is why a polite society tacitly agrees not to look too close.

As a teenager I had not yet learned that rule, or at least I still dared to break it. I had been taught all my life, *don't stare,* so maybe it was a subtle form of rebellion that my friends and I played a game we called Stare Dare. The object was to look into each other's eyes as long as possible until somebody couldn't stand it anymore and had to look away. It's harder than it sounds. At first you can hardly keep from laughing but then this sort of unease and seriousness sets in. You feel a kind of vulnerability, like you're naked in a way you've never been before, and you realize the eyes really are the window to the soul. This person can see *into* me, into what I *really am.*

Sometimes I wished I could see what my friends saw in my eyes. I wanted to see what I really am. I wanted to see my soul. Sometimes I thought I could because on rare occasions when I stared into a mirror, the eyes that stared back seemed different than my own. They seemed to hold a knowledge beyond my own. They seemed to divulge my entire future, to assure me of all the wonders yet to come. I saw a life far removed from humdrum routine. I saw passion and intrigue. I would sail even farther than the seven seas. My life would be one long string of adventures and romance, but not merely with a knight in shining armor. Rather, I would find a deep, profound love, a love that would reach to the depths of our souls.

In those mirror eyes I saw that my life would be more than I had ever dreamed; I was more than the skin and bones that would someday grow old and die. I saw a woman with a unique purpose in this world, a purpose that only I could fulfill. My life would have meaning because who I am truly mattered. Oh, how I had wanted to believe what I saw reflected in the mirror way back then.

As I finish applying the last eyeshadow that I'll wear for forty days, I dare myself to look straight into the eyes of the thirty-one-year-old that I have become, as if I might, just once more, catch a glimpse of my soul. If I did, I would demand an explanation. I would demand to know what happened to that bright future that was so certainly mine. I'd demand to know what that business of a unique purpose was all about.

Looking into the mirror now, however, I see eyes filled not with assurance and promise but with uncertainty and trepidation. I'm not surprised. If it were as easy as looking in a mirror, my problems would have been solved long ago. If the soul answered to command performances, I wouldn't be going to the desert. Maybe it's not possible to summon one's soul at all, but maybe it's a matter of what a person is willing to do to find it. I have to believe that. I'm willing to risk my life on the chance that sometimes that's what it takes.

❧

The aisles at the supermarket are empty, and the only two people in sight—a box boy and a cashier—eye me with suspicion. It could be the way I'm dressed. A blue print bandanna covers every trace of my hair except my bangs, and I bought my jeans and flannel shirt from a thrift shop. Maybe they're just curious because most people don't shop at 4:30 in the morning, two hours before the sun will peek over the Wasatch range to bathe Salt Lake City in morning's glow. The box boy pushing a mop doesn't look up as I pass by.

"Could you point me to the bottled water?"

"Three aisles over."

The market is festive in pre-Thanksgiving celebration. Paper turkeys with orange and brown tissue tail feathers dangle from the ceiling. Pumpkins and cornstalks adorn the checkout lanes.

I turn into the aisle. The floor still glistens from its recent mop job. I spot the water midway down, but as I approach it a tiny flash of fur darts in front of me. I catch my breath. *Mouse.* When I was three years old, just before my sisters—twins—were born, my parents and I lived in a tiny bedroom-and-a-half university apartment. Dad was working on his Ph.D. in genetics, studying field mice, which he kept in a cage in the only available space in the apartment—my half-bedroom. That was also where he kept his snakes, to dispose of his used mice, I suppose. And I've always been afraid of both.

A shiver runs down my spine as the rodent disappears into a space between the shelves. I wish I hadn't seen it, for it only reminds me that on a scale of one to ten—one being brave, ten being an absolute coward—I peg out at about twelve. The desert is one of the few remaining natural habitats of the mountain lion. If a mouse sends my heart pounding, how will I cope with real danger?

I wheel my cart in front of the bottled water and begin to load up. I've calculated that a gallon a day is enough, but to be on the safe side I add another half gallon a day. Four jugs remain on the shelf and I grab those as well. The cart is so heavy that the wheels squeak against the linoleum as I steer toward the checkout counter. I think of the homeless and toothless old women I've seen on the streets of New York City, pushing their stolen shopping carts loaded with all of their worldly possessions, cast by fate into a type of emptiness from which one never recovers.

"What in the world?" The clerk's name tag reads Wanda.

She calls to the box boy. "Scotty, get your tail-end over here. Can't you see we need some help? Honey, where are you goin' with all that water? Nobody told me about no drought."

"Camping," I say.

"Must be some trip," Wanda says, staring at the cart. "Whatcha got—a whole army to look after?"

"I'm going alone."

"Taking your Jacuzzi, eh?" She laughs, poking the box boy with her elbow.

"This has to last me forty days," I say. "I'm going to the desert."

Her laughter freezes along with her fingers in midair above the cash register. "Forty days? Alone? Lord, girl, what's the matter with you? It's dangerous out there."

"Aren't you scared?" the box boy asks.

"A little," I answer. A twelve.

"You got a gun, don't you?" Wanda says, her eyes widening by the second.

"No."

"Short-wave radio?" the box boy asks.

"No."

"No cell phone?" Wanda says. "No way anyone can reach you? Now *that* I could go for. Forty days without hearing from the bank. It's not like this job pays enough to keep my family's head above water. I'm afraid to even answer the phone anymore. Honey, I'd give a fair chunk of change to trade places with you."

I hand the clerk a fifty-dollar bill, but it is my face that she studies. If I don't look away she will see beneath the surface, she will see the storm hurling me like a tin can in a tornado. I want to break her gaze, but then I notice that her eyes are green. Another chill runs down my spine as I remember other eyes, eyes that not so long ago looked so deeply into mine that they seemed to see everything that I am. I didn't want to hide anything from those eyes.

Suddenly I wish I didn't have to hide anything from Wanda, either. I wish I could find the words to explain why I'm going to the desert for forty days, to a place almost as foreign to me as the moon. If I could tell her all that has happened, if I could tell her the most intimate details of my life, I would. Maybe she'd understand and then I wouldn't feel so lonely. I wouldn't be so afraid. But I can't find those words.

It has always amazed me that Henry David Thoreau captured the entire intent of his isolation at Walden Pond in just six little words: *Because I wished to live deliberately.* Six words that perfectly illuminated the nobility of his goal and the strength of his determination. Six words that anyone who refused to lead a life of quiet desperation could cling to for hope that another way indeed existed. Six words that conveyed one man's utter conviction that the fact that we live and breathe is such a miracle, it would be an insult to our very existence if we did not sit still to watch and ponder our place in all that surrounds us.

But I have also always wondered what else was really behind those six words, what else really prompted Thoreau to spend two years in the woods. Some people scoff that he walked to town by day and entertained visitors by night, but still he must have been more solitary than his contemporaries, and surely more so than mine. If he had been lucky in love, or if the school he'd started with his brother hadn't gone belly up; if he hadn't ended up, essentially, as Emerson's handyman, would Thoreau have felt the same need? It couldn't have been easy in Emerson's shadow as audiences clamored to read the master's works and stood in line to hear him speak, while Thoreau watched from the wings.

I've wondered if there was a certain moment when he threw up his hands and said *that's it.* Maybe he couldn't figure out exactly what quality Emerson had that he didn't. Despite his legendary bravado, Thoreau may not have understood why he felt different from everyone else, why he couldn't bring himself to get a steady job beyond that offered by his father in the family's pencil factory. Despite his criticism that the Concord townspeople led shallow and—by his standards—meaningless lives, perhaps Thoreau wondered if his own life had any more purpose and meaning than theirs. Maybe he even feared he would never be happy.

I know the feeling. It's terrifying.

James—we married in 1982, a week before my nineteenth birthday—once told our marriage counselor that he didn't think I could be happy. He told her that he wasn't even sure I wanted to be happy. Imagine that. A person who doesn't want happiness.

No matter how good things were, James said, I always found something lacking. He provided for our family—his daughter Gina from a previous marriage and our son Tony—sixty grand–plus a year. We had a two-story house a mile from the beach in central California, two cars, nice clothes, money to put me through college. I graduated with a liberal arts degree after twice changing majors. First I thought I wanted to be a teacher; at the time both my parents taught at an American school in Taiwan, Dad science and Mom language arts. Then I thought I wanted to work in city government. I had also worked in an office supply company and then as an office manager for a real estate firm.

"She could stay home with the kids," James told the counselor, "but she says that doesn't fulfill her. Nothing fulfills her. I think she expects too much."

I wondered if maybe I did. That would explain everything, including the first time in our marriage I apparently held too-high expectations: My first attempt to cook Thanksgiving dinner, fifteen months after we married. At twenty years old I'd never cooked anything even approximating the bulk of a turkey before, and I didn't dare try. I scoured the magazines looking for the perfect recipe, and finally the solution appeared, pictured in full color: Cornish rock hens with sage thyme dressing. I followed the instructions to the letter, and by noon Thanksgiving Day, even Julia Child would have approved of the aroma simmering in my oven.

"Where's *dinner?*" James said as I placed the delicate feast on the table. "Where's the turkey?"

I had hoped he would say something like, "Cornish rock hens? How clever you are, my dear. It's just like you to try something new. Your creativity makes me love you all the more each day."

But he didn't.

"Next time just cook a turkey, OK? Like Mom does, OK?"

Maybe I did want too much. Maybe I expected too much from the man I trusted to bolster my self-image instead of shatter it. But I felt something happen inside me that day. I felt myself pull away from him, like somebody had reached into the bathtub and yanked the plug, only it was a much slower drain.

Within a year James's daughter, Gina, came to live with us. Two years later Tony was born. By then James and I had achieved what might be called a marriage of utility. We discussed the children. We paid the bills. We argued and we made up. He golfed on Saturday, while I and the other golf wives prepared an afternoon barbecue. When the guys returned, they played pool in the garage and rehashed their game play by play while we wives sat in the kitchen and talked about whose kid had just lost his first tooth.

"It's like we're living some kind of charade, going through the motions," I told the marriage counselor after James and I had been married eight years. "I'm twenty-seven years old and I feel like . . . this is *it?* I want more from life."

"She wants something that doesn't exist," James said.

I was beginning to suspect he was right, because the life I had seen reflected in my eyes in the mirror years before had not materialized. Passion and intrigue belonged to the soap operas. My unique purpose revolved around making sure my family had clean underwear in their drawers. Thanks to my parents, I had at least sailed a few seas. James and I visited them once in Asia, and another summer we joined them in Italy. But on our own we wouldn't have taken either trip. When James refused their third invitation, I knew our travel days were over. Slowly I began to fear that the life and love I had imagined for myself were just that: imaginations.

A year later, in 1991, I heard about a postgraduate editing seminar in Denver. I had been working on a freelance basis for some of my former college professors editing their texts before publication. Formal certification would add to my credentials, and I thought I was on the way to finding a satisfying occupation, albeit a low-paying one. James agreed to hold down the household while I attended the month-long course at Denver University.

Most of the hundred participants were just out of college, and at twenty-eight I was among the oldest. We were housed in dorms. Having not started college until after I married, I hadn't lived on campus since that bedroom-and-a-half apartment when I was three years old. I had never once eaten in a university cafeteria. Now I did so, three very delicious meals a day. Food that had been prepared for me. Dishes I didn't have to wash. Not a bad deal.

Going out for a beer after studying until ten was par for the course for those who had gone straight from high school to college, but for me it was a whole different world. I went out every weekend with my classmates, barely making it back before the dorm's doors locked for curfew at two. Once, we didn't return until two-thirty, and we had to climb up the ivy to sneak in through a second-story window, a plan I hadn't considered wise since I was about sixteen. As for other extracurricular activities, I was one of the few who had brought along a car, so I was never short on takers for a free lift to Boulder or Colorado Springs or into the Rockies.

I'd never had so much fun in my life. I felt like a whole new woman. And each day I felt more guilty.

"Miss you too," I'd say when James called, and then I'd cringe as I forced the words from my throat. "Yeah, love you too."

The days passed in a blur and before I knew it, three weeks of the seminar were gone. It was Friday afternoon. I remember it clearly because I was anxious for the weekend, the last weekend before the last five days of the seminar. I was picturing an ice-cold beer at the summit of Pikes Peak when the director introduced the final speaker of the day, Jerry Ellis, a writer from Alabama.

Part Cherokee, Jerry had walked the same route, but in reverse, across the eight states that his ancestors had followed in the heart of the winter of 1838 during their forced evacuation to Indian Territory in Oklahoma, the nine-hundred-mile journey known as the Trail of Tears. By following their path in reverse, he meant to honor those ancestors and symbolically return their souls to their original homelands. Jerry's book about the journey, *Walking the Trail,* had earned him a nomination for the Pulitzer Prize.

"The first night out," Jerry lectured from the podium, "I had blisters on my feet so bad I thought I'd never walk again. But that first night was the only time I had doubts. I was forced to depend on the strength of my mind as well as my body to keep me moving. All along the way I met people who reminded me that not everyone values the almighty dollar above all else. Walking alone, day after day, I got more in touch with who I am and my understanding of God. By the end of that trip, I no longer questioned myself. I had done something I believed in with all my soul."

As I heard his words, all thoughts of weekend celebrations disappeared. I couldn't make out Jerry's features, I was sitting so far in the rear of the room, but the word *soul* cut through me like a knife. My heart began to pound as if I myself had run the same nine hundred miles he walked. I didn't understand why my hands went cold or why my head went dizzy. But I did understand, in one single moment, that I hadn't been wrong.

My *soul* hadn't been wrong. It *is* possible to experience more in life than humdrum routine. Not a hundred feet away stood a man who felt the sense of purpose and meaning that I had always wanted for myself. He had found it because he had listened to his *soul.*

I wasn't the only one who wanted to meet Jerry. I waited for an hour to shake his hand, hardly noticing the time, hardly noticing that the line slowly dwindled until I was the only one left, hardly recognizing my own voice when I asked him to dinner.

"This is your *house?*" I held the picture that Jerry pulled from his wallet closer to the candle that lit the table at the funky downtown Denver restaurant. The wine served in jelly jars—his red, mine white—matched the checkered tablecloth. "You're kidding. It started out as a tree house?"

"My father and I built it seven years ago with my nephew," Jerry said. "The next year I built down to the ground and added a fireplace. Actually, I use it more for a retreat. It doesn't have electricity or running water."

"It looks like a big kid's dream come true. And where is this?"

"Fort Payne, in the northeastern corner of Alabama. My folks bought two hundred acres back in the fifties. That's where I grew up. Even though I've lived all over the States, no other place could be home. I guess that's where I'll die."

The wine warmed in my stomach, and a gentle haze floated from my cigarette to mingle with the candle's smoke as Janis Joplin softly strummed in the background. James, I knew, would despise this place, but I never wanted to leave.

"You're not married?" I asked.

"Once, back when I was in college," Jerry nodded. "She traded me in for the next year's model—that's about how long it lasted. A couple of times since I thought I found the right woman but . . . I'm not so sure she's really out there."

"She is." I wondered if he'd laugh at me for sounding so certain but no trace of a smile crossed his lips.

"How do you know?" he said.

"I just do."

Jerry's eyes sparkled and for the first time I noticed their color, as green as the sea and flecked with gold that shimmered in the candlelight. "Thankfully, at least one of us knows true love."

"Me? Oh. I guess so. We've been married almost nine years."

"But you're not happy." It was neither a question nor an accusation; rather, it was a simple statement of fact, as simple as if Jerry had said that my eyes were brown, which they are. I realized I'd been staring into his eyes far longer than could be dismissed as casual observation. But he hadn't looked away.

"James says being happy isn't in my repertoire," I said, forcing a little laugh, forcing myself to concentrate on my finger, tracing the outline of the checkered cloth. "He says I want something that doesn't exist."

"It exists," Jerry said.

"How do you know?"

"I just do."

I searched his eyes for some sign that he meant to mock me, but I only felt pulled further into their depths. He reached across the table and touched his fingers to my cheek. When he spoke his tone was so soft that it occurred to me I'd never heard such tenderness expressed by anyone before. "What you're looking for is real. Maybe it's a matter of what you're willing to do to find it."

"I would do anything," I said, barely above a whisper.

"I believe you."

At that moment, I believed myself. I felt flung into a living dream where anything was possible, even happiness, even for a lifetime, even for me. But I wasn't thinking about a lifetime. Only that night mattered. Seven nights later I would go back to my family, to what I was and would always be. I would go on as if Denver never existed, as if I had never met a man who had listened to his soul, as if I had never believed for just one night that life could be even more than I had ever dared to dream.

At the time I hardly noticed the flicker in Jerry's eyes as he held my stare, as if he sensed something in my future that I could not. Two days later I found a copy of *Walden Pond* on my pillow in the dorm room. On the inside cover he'd inscribed: *There are a thousand ways to go to the Woods. Someday you'll find yours.*

Three years later I still wonder how he knew.

"I wish you luck," Wanda says, handing me my change as Scotty the box boy lugs the last gallon of water into my shopping cart. I blink as if I've been in another world, and perhaps I have. "Maybe someday I'll do something like you are, for whatever reason you're doing it."

I could simply say, "I'm going to the desert because I wish to live deliberately." Six little words borrowed from a man who managed to say it all. Six little words from someone who broke free of his mentor's shadow, who carved out his own identity, who did not go to his grave with his purpose unfulfilled.

And yet I hesitate, remembering the green eyes flecked with gold that once took me to the deepest part of myself, a place where

I was not afraid to show someone else exactly who I am, a place I fear I may never reach again. Perhaps that is why I now tell Wanda the truth.

"I'm going to the desert," I say, "because if I don't I think a part of me will die."

"What part?" The clerk's tone is as gentle as a mother to a child, as if she somehow knows that I'm revealing the most intimate secret of my life.

"The part that believes in my soul."

She reaches across the cash register to cover my hand, and I can't hold back the rest.

"I'm so tired of hurting," I say. "I've tried everything else I can think of. I don't mean to imply that I'm anything like them, but when Moses and Muhammad and Christ faced turning points in their lives, they went to the desert to ask . . . to ask God what they should do. Sometimes I'm sure God has a purpose for me. But if he does, I can't figure out what it is. I've hurt the people I love the most and if there's not a reason . . ."

"It's quiet in the desert," Wanda says. Her voice is kind, without a trace of judgment. "Sometimes we can only hear our answers, no matter where they come from, in a quiet place. While you're out there, try to remember that you're not alone. We all wonder what life's all about—at least those of us who bother to think from time to time. You don't think I have my doubts? Most of us just don't have the courage to face them."

"It's not courage," I say, shaking my head as I push the cart toward the door. The wheels squeak so loudly that I don't know if she hears my final words. "It's desperation."

Chapter Two

The sunrise is lovely in its pinks and blues over the Wasatch range as I cruise south on I-15 out of Salt Lake City, stopping at a McDonald's for an egg and cheese biscuit. I savor each bite between sips of Diet Coke. Neither item will show up on my desert menu.

I exit at Lehi and head due west on a state road. Ten miles later, civilization as most people know it ceases, replaced by dark rocky fields as far as the eye can see. The human touch, however, is evident in the wooden fence posts strung one to the next with barbed wire and the occasional gate locked tight with heavy chains.

I decide to play a game called Count the Fence Posts because I can't get my mind off the fact that somebody had to dig all those post holes, and I wonder how long it took. I count 157 before I notice a cowboy boot shoved over one of the posts. At least that confirms I brought appropriate footwear. I checked the thrift shop for hiking boots as a backup for my Reeboks but all they had was one pair of leather cowboy boots. Fit like gloves, which I also bought at the thrift store.

The only items I purchased new are an air mattress, an ax and a staple gun, not including the lumber and the tarps that I bought at a discount hardware store, which I'll use to construct my shelter. Forty days is too long to sleep in a tent but I'm not much of a carpenter, so I'll use my tent until I can build the shelter.

My car—I call her Betsy—is a Ford Escort, two-door hatchback, not four-wheel drive, and she has never been so loaded. Sixty-four gallons of water is the tip of the iceberg. Food, a campstove, a lantern, two-dozen propane canisters, my clothes. Dish towels, a frying pan, a soup pot, first-aid kit, camera and a box of craft supplies. Hammer, saw, sleeping bags, kitchen utensils and a bag of newspapers for starting campfires.

My parents are among the few people I know who wouldn't balk at how limited my gear really is. After Dad received his doctorate, we moved to Tacoma, Washington, an hour's drive from the heart of the Cascades. A not-yet-tenured university professor with a family and a mortgage payment doesn't have much money to throw around during the summer breaks. For entertainment we camped.

We camped in state parks and national parks and in no parks. We camped by lakes and rivers and where there was no water at all. We camped as a family and with other families and with my grandparents, and one summer Mom took just us girls.

Once my parents packed us up for a three-week trek into the Canadian wilderness by canoe. I'll always remember that trip because that's when Mom discovered dehydrated scrambled eggs and an even greater novelty—dehydrated ice cream. It's also where I counted more than a hundred mosquito bites on my body at one time. Maybe that's where I got the idea to count fence posts.

Another summer we followed Lewis and Clark's journey, albeit in reverse, down the Missouri River. Dad brought a copy of their journal. So precise were their descriptions and so little had the area changed that we found some of the exact spots where the expedition had camped. With no facilities anywhere nearby, at each new spot we dug a hole a hundred yards from camp and set a potty chair on stilts atop it. Better than squatting when you're in rattlesnake country, but even so I wouldn't go alone, terrified that a coiled rattler lurked under every stone.

Mom made our tents out of a parachute she had bought at the Army Surplus. Dad designed a reflector oven out of cookie sheets. Propped in front of the campfire, it baked like a charm. We picked huckleberries all afternoon and ate fresh cobbler at night as the other campers sniffed the air wondering where that sweet smell was coming from. Didn't cost us hardly a dime.

We used to shake our heads at the folks who passed us on the trail with their $200 hiking boots and $300 insulated sleeping bags and $400 backpacks. As if Daniel Boone paid a fortune for his hat, we'd say. As if Lewis and Clark spent a million bucks on their deerskin coats. *That's not camping,* we'd say, *that's cheating.*

And I believed it with all my heart. It only now occurs to me that whenever we called sophisticated gear "cheating," my parents looked at each other in a funny sort of way. They never let on that they wished they could afford the swanky stuff. They were doing the best they could, and I never had a clue that they wished anything about our life was different.

Just now I wish I had someone to look at in a funny sort of way. I wish I could afford the latest in desert survival gear—hiking boots, insulated rain garb, the whole works. I'm doing the best I can. Just now I wish everything was different.

❦

I pull to the side of the highway when I see the sign. Bret Layman, the naturalist who will haul me and my supplies the final miles into isolation, told me where to look or I'd miss it, its letters are so faded. Pony Express Route, it says, and points to a one-lane dirt road. Eighty miles from here is the wildlife refuge where Bret works as a ranger. It's another eighty miles beyond the Refuge to the Gosiute Indian Reservation, on the Nevada border. Bret and his girlfriend, Dana, live at the Refuge. No one commutes into the desert.

It's all dirt road from here. Bret said it's not much smoother than the original Pony Express tracks. I check my gas gauge. My last chance to fill the tank was twenty miles ago. The desert unfolds before me as I leave the pavement behind. Flat. Sand made white by the concentration of saline, marred only by rocky ridges that surge thousands of feet above the valley floor like ships on an open sea. Now all signs of civilization vanish save the occasional crumbling foundations of the original Pony Express stations. No telephone poles. No electric wires. No other cars.

The Great Basin, as this region is called, contains fewer life forms than any other North American desert. Absent are many species of cactus, yucca and agave. In western Utah, sagebrush dominates the scene with a few other hardy plants, among them shadscale. Where shadscale is prominent, so is livestock, but not the riotous herds of cattle found to the north in Wyoming. Sheep, mostly. As always, the problem is water.

Will sixty-four gallons quench my thirst for forty days?

A herd of antelope, spooked by the dust spewing from Betsy's wheels, darts away, first becoming specks and then becoming completely lost in the white sands of the horizon. I wonder if the animals are aware that as they run, the land beneath them is also moving. Literally. The earth's crust that underlies the Great Basin is slowly stretching. During my lifetime Reno and Salt Lake City will separate by about one human pace. Over the past eight million years the cities have moved fifty miles apart. The earth's crust here is some of the thinnest on the globe. Someday, geologists say, the stretching will open up an ocean, right where I'm driving.

The *desert*. It is at once the most exciting and frightening place I've ever been. Some call it the land of enchantment, others the land of mystery—both labels are accurate. In the past three years I've traveled through much of America's wilderness areas and experienced virtually all of its different terrains, from the swamplands of Louisiana to the great prairies of Kansas and Nebraska, from the spectacular changing of the fall colors in New England to the brilliant splendor of spring cherry blossoms in Washington D.C., from the waves pounding against the jagged coast at Big Sur, California, to the surf lapping against the outer banks of North Carolina. In the past three years Betsy and I have driven to all forty-eight of the continental United States and nine of the Canadian provinces. My odyssey began in the desert; for all I know it began because of the desert. This very desert.

I crossed it for the first time in 1991, en route from California to the postgraduate publishing seminar in Denver.

Until that day I had never even seen the Mojave, the first of the deserts I would encounter along the way. It loomed like a giant sandpit of terror just beyond Barstow, California. A seventy-five foot neon-lit thermometer—the world's largest, or so it claimed—in Baker, ninety miles further into the desert, registered 105 degrees at nine in the morning. I chugged along at forty-five miles an hour

to spare Betsy's engine every inch of that seemingly endless waste-
land, awed by the eerie, spindly branches of the Joshua trees.

I had no wish to linger in the Mojave. By instinct I knew that
humans do not belong in the desert, not without the safety of
technology. Air conditioners, irrigation and water diversion make
it possible, but if I had to face the desert on its own terms, I would
lose.

I breathed easier when I reached Las Vegas and sped on toward Utah, first passing through Arizona's Virgin River Gorge
before turning north. Upon entering Utah, I began to see road signs
for Zion and Bryce Canyon National Parks. Ever since I was a kid
I'd heard my dad talk about how he rode on the back of a mule
from Bryce's rim down to the bottom, where giant red rock forma-
tions looked like ghosts frozen in stone. I had always wanted to see
those ghosts, but my family never had the money to make the trip.

Now that I'd finally made it to Utah I knew I might never be
back. Now might be my only chance, but the parks were not on
the interstate. To avoid a four-hour backtrack I'd have to take a
state road—marked on the map as a thread-thin black line—
through virtual desert wilderness.

I saw the sign for Zion. Exit, one-half mile. "Do it," a voice
within me urged.

I didn't have the courage for that kind of chance. Otherwise
dependable cars break down in the desert—I'd passed about a dozen
of them in the Mojave. Hoods raised, hazard lights flashing, steam
billowing. Nobody seemed to stop to offer assistance, including
me, but every half mile or so there were emergency call boxes.
Even half a mile is a long walk when it's 105 degrees at nine in the
morning, and I was sure that there would be no emergency call
boxes along the state roads. What if I had to walk ten or twenty

miles for help through the rattlesnake-infested wilderness? Maybe the heat would get me and I'd go crazy. Maybe a madman would find me first. Maybe anything.

Zion Exit, one-quarter mile ahead. Stay the course.

I still can't explain why I swerved off the interstate at the last possible second. At first I was so scared I could hardly keep my foot on the gas pedal. My mind screamed at me, *danger, danger!* I wanted to turn around, get back to the highway, get back to where it was safe, but I didn't. Half an hour later Betsy hadn't broken down. An hour later she still hadn't, and I began to believe that maybe she wouldn't. I felt a freedom I had never experienced before. No one at home knew where I was. No one in the desert knew who I was. That day I answered to no one.

With the windows rolled down and the stereo turned up, I discovered why cars come equipped with third gear—that's what Betsy stayed in as we scooted up high desert mountain roads so steep and narrow I could only pray that no one else as equally bit by the adventure bug was headed our way. Rock towers looking just like the ghosts my father had described jutted into the sky while high-topped mesas, void of human footprints, sprawled across the desert floor. My hair tousled into a tangled mess as my bangs slapped against my forehead. I didn't care.

Time stopped. Everything ceased to exist except the music and the desert and the heat and the wind and . . . and me. Me. That day I discovered that there really is more to me than the woman I had come to accept as myself. I discovered that somewhere inside there was a woman who wasn't too afraid to veer off the beaten path, to take a chance. A different woman drove out of the desert than had driven in.

I've always wondered what would have happened if I hadn't

taken that exit off the interstate. If the desert hadn't touched me then, would I be returning to it now? I can only pray that its power is real. If I emerge in forty days unchanged, my purpose will be defeated.

Bret Layman wasn't kidding when he claimed that this road is little better than the original Pony Express trail. I try to steer clear of the potholes, but there are too many and I can't see them soon enough. The road climbs up the side of a wash and then suddenly drops into another and then up again. The sixty-four gallons of water bounce in manic rhythm, a beat that matches my heart.

I'm relieved when, after more than two hours on the dirt road, silvery-green rushes confirm the edge of a shallow saline marsh that Bret said marks the eastern boundary of the wildlife refuge. I'll find the office and barracks ten miles farther in the heart of the refuge.

Only a few clouds graze the sky. I touch a lighter to my cigarette and crack my window an inch. A breeze rustles over my bandanna and my bangs tickle my forehead, reminding me of my first crossing of the desert three years ago. The bangs are the longest part of my hairstyle. I've worn it short for ten years, but I asked the stylist to cut it extra brief for my retreat. As I did the day I left Denver in 1991. A shiver passes through my body, but not from the cold. From the memory.

Jerry didn't say good-bye when he left Denver to return to Alabama. I supposed it was better that way. I hadn't even known what I would say.

I lay in bed for three days explaining to the seminar's director that I didn't feel well. In truth I felt worse than I'd ever felt in my life. I felt as if a giant crack had opened down the center of my chest, pulling me apart until I would surely break.

How could I return to a marriage that wasn't a marriage? Even if I was willing to be miserable—and actually, I was willing—no matter how hard I tried to pretend, I knew I didn't love James. Not the way a man deserves to be loved. No matter how hard I tried to deceive myself, James and I weren't really married, not in the way people who truly love each other are. Marriage isn't a certificate. It isn't only a commitment to stay together come hell or high water. It is a promise to "love and honor," and I couldn't make myself love James any more than I could make him love me more and more each day.

But how could divorce be a better alternative? In my entire family's history there had only been one divorce, my uncle's. My grandfather—Dad's dad—as old school as they come, was devastated, but at least there were no children involved. I already knew what divorce would mean for my kids.

A year earlier, on the advice of our marriage counselor, James and I had separated for four months. Because I couldn't take both children—Gina, my stepdaughter, would stay with her father—and because we didn't want to split the children up, I was the one who left while both kids stayed with James. He hired a housekeeper who managed the household far more smoothly than I ever had. She took the kids to school, did all the laundry and cleaning and shopping, and was home when the kids returned from school. But we all knew it was a temporary separation. After four months I came back, not for my marriage's sake but because I couldn't bear the thought of tearing a family to pieces.

I couldn't bear the thought of being without my son.

What kind of mother would separate her son from his sister and father and from his own bed in his own bedroom? For what? So he could live in a tiny apartment with me, supported by whatever income the courts decreed his father should provide? What kind of selfishness would drive a mother to that?

And yet, is a mother a good mother if she's a liar? That's what I would be. Our lives would be a sham.

But James said he was happy. I was the one with the problem, and I had no right to shatter his life.

I lay in that Denver dorm room, tossing and turning into the pillow as the birds chirped outside the open window and a sprinkler watered the lawn. No matter what I chose, I would lose. But now I knew that I must choose or the chasm in my chest would never close. I had to choose for us all.

I had to go back. I couldn't live with myself if I didn't.

I would return to my family, a family oblivious to the destruction that was almost their fate. The years would go by, my hair would turn gray, and before I knew it I would look in the mirror and wonder how the lines got on my face. Gina and Tony would grow up and move away and get married and have children of their own. They'd come home for Thanksgiving and I'd roast a turkey just as I'd done every year since the second year of my marriage. I would get old and I would go to my death knowing that I had done the right thing.

The liar would live a long and noble life. Who I am would die that day in the Denver dorm room. I knew that as surely as I'd ever known anything. The life I had seen for myself in my teenage eyes, a life I now knew was possible, would never come to be.

Suddenly I knew something else: I couldn't do it. I couldn't do what I had to do. Not for James. Not for my stepdaughter. Not for my son. Not for God. I couldn't abandon my soul. I just couldn't.

The sprinkler outside the window had long ago stopped and the setting sun had sent the birds back to their nests when I finally crawled from bed and reached for the phone.

"James?" I said when the familiar voice answered. "James, I'm sorry. We have to talk."

Ten minutes later I had spared us all from one fate and condemned us all to another. But as of that August evening in 1991, I would no longer call myself a liar.

I didn't know what to do then, so I took a walk. I noticed an open beauty parlor. I went inside and asked the stylist to cut my hair short.

Chapter Three

I've never had much luck telling time by the sun, and as Betsy and I traverse the last few miles to the wildlife refuge, I wish that Betsy had a clock or that I wore a watch. In my haste I managed to leave the travel alarm clock on the motel room bedstand—not that keeping time will be necessary for the next forty days. When I called Bret Layman from Salt Lake City yesterday, I told him I'd arrive at the wildlife refuge sometime before noon. I look forward to meeting the ranger. Thus far we've only spoken by phone.

Born and raised in the Utah desert, Bret knows the entire area like the back of his hand. The only problem, he told me, is that there aren't many spots with enough firewood to sustain a campfire for forty days, and desert nights can get chilly in November and December. But he did know of a canyon on land administered by the Bureau of Land Management. Anyone can enter public lands, but tenancy is typically limited to fourteen days unless the BLM grants a special permit. It was unlikely they'd grant me one, he had said, given my refusal to carry a weapon or a communication device.

As far as Bret knew, however, the limit didn't apply to this particular canyon because the government hadn't yet classified it as a threatened environment. Yes, he would take me there. All I had to do was get myself to the wildlife refuge. He'd truck me in and return forty days later to truck me out.

"Sure you don't want to take a gun?" Bret asked before hanging up. "I got an extra pistol you're welcome to borrow."

I don't want a pistol. I don't want a radio. Neither were available to Christ or Moses or Muhammad. To my knowledge, of course, none of them had brought a forty-day supply of food and water, nor had they brought lumber, tarps and a cookstove. Perhaps those prophets would look at my pile of gear and say that I'm *cheating*. Maybe so. Maybe because they were born and bred in the desert they were naturally equipped to take care of themselves, or perhaps God looked upon them so favorably that He waived their normal bodily requirements. I am hardly of that status on either count.

When I finally turn off the dirt road onto the gravel driveway of the wildlife refuge, I find Bret and Dana waiting on the office steps. The only other vehicle in the parking lot is a Toyota truck, once white but now layered with grime.

"Have any trouble finding the place?" Bret asks, wiping his hand on his coveralls before extending it toward mine.

"Looks like you're ready for a real romp in the wild," Dana says as she and Bret help me transfer my supplies into their truck. She holds a carton of cigarettes in the air. "Not giving up smoking, huh? Seems like the perfect time."

"Not a chance," I say. Simplicity is one thing. Torture is another.

Bret grins as he tightens a tarp over the truck. I take a long last look at Betsy. *Oh, my unfailing companion, I'll miss you. You've carried me everywhere I wanted to go, back and forth across the country, up and down the nation's coasts. Now I must leave you behind. Even if you could survive the journey off road, I don't dare trust myself to resist the option your presence would allow.*

"You wouldn't know it by looking," Bret says as we pull out of the wildlife refuge, "but this road has changed the whole ecology of the area from the days of the Pony Express. Even minor human interference can wipe out a species that's lived for centuries in balance. More and more folks are looking to the desert for recreation. They run all over with their all-terrain vehicles. Maybe they don't know that the sagebrush they trample took twenty years to grow. Will it grow back? Depends on whether it's seeded. Chances are good it won't. The recreationers don't care about one little sagebrush, but I've lived here all my life, and those sage are adding up. The desert's changing faster than I can keep track."

"I bet you can't imagine living anywhere else," I say.

"No, I can't," Bret says, "but it's not an easy life. Especially for Dana. At least I've got my work."

"I'd go crazy without the television," Dana says. "Thank God we've got electricity and running water. Some folks out here don't even have that. There's no grocery store, no gas station, no restaurant. Wouldn't matter if we had money, there's no place to spend it. Even the post office is only open twice a week. If the weather is bad the mail stops altogether."

"Trouble is," Bret adds, "there's not many ways to make a living off the desert. My sister and mother live in Calleo, thirty miles from here. My sister quarries rock for landscaping. Little pieces of Utah end up all over the country."

"A lot of folks get welfare," Dana says, "but some would rather die than accept money from the government. Most people out here want to live as they see fit. Like the Squirrel Man."

"Who?"

"We call him that because he hunts squirrels to eat," Dana explains.

"His real name's Fred," Bret says. "Fought in Vietnam. Didn't want to go, hated fighting, but his number came up and off he went. From day one he tried to figure a way out. Took him until he'd been there long enough to fall in love with a Vietnamese woman. He was desperate to get her out of the war zone. So he shot a soldier. In the ass. Thing is, it was an American ass. He got his discharge, a dishonorable one at that, but Fred didn't care. He just wanted to bring his bride home.

"The government's wheels grind a little slower for those who shoot at our own boys, though, and Fred waited two years and cleared a hundred hurdles before his wife finally stepped off the plane onto American soil. The day she did was the last time he laid his loving eyes upon her. All she'd wanted was a free ride to the promised land. He never got over it. To this day Fred blames the government for shipping him off to 'Nam in the first place.

"After that, he refused to have anything to do with anything governmental. He moved to a satellite parcel of a friend's ranch outside Calleo, about an acre of land, right near a stream. Watercress grows wild in the bogs, and that's the staple of his diet when the squirrel population runs low. But he won't shoot a deer. That'd be poaching."

"Everybody's tried to help him," Dana says. "All the ranchers have offered him work. He won't do nothing, though. Says if he earned an income, it'd be illegal for him not to pay taxes, and he won't break no laws but he's determined not to pay the government a dime. He'd be damned before he'd tell anybody his Social Security number. We don't know how he gets his essentials. Everybody's got to have toothpaste and toilet paper, maybe a little cooking oil. He stays with us for a night or two every now and then. I always try to sneak a bar of soap into his pocket."

Their compassion reminds me that neither of them have asked my reasons for spending forty days in the desert. Perhaps it's because they don't need to. Perhaps Bret and Dana are aware that I too am willing to pay a price to seek out my answers in freedom.

Nonetheless, I wonder if others who reside in this harsh land will respect my wish. Who else lives here? Rattlesnake Man? Badger Man? Who among them may have turned to darkness and evil, so disillusioned that a lone woman is merely a target for rage? Bret and Dana can lock their doors against those who comprise the underbelly of the desert's inhabitants, as sure to exist in this semblance of society as in any other, despite my effort to leave all of society behind. I will have no locks. I will be completely vulnerable save for the most primitive weapons: an ax and my wits. But that is my choice.

Bret swings the truck off the dirt road onto what appear to be two faded tire tracks in the otherwise virgin ground. "If you should get into trouble," he says, pointing to a large, spindly shrub, "you can hike down from the canyon and tie a flag of surveyor's tape on this bush. We'll drive by every few days, and if we see the ribbon we'll know to come after you."

"How far is the canyon?" I ask.

"Five miles."

Despite my desire to rely solely on myself, the contingency plan makes sense, though if I'm in good enough shape to trek five miles through the desert to a bush and five miles back I probably don't need help bad enough to hike to it. But what if I *can't* hike for help?

We head toward a range of rocky ridges that spill into the desert floor about two miles away.

"You said you wanted remote," Bret yells above the bouncing Toyota. "You'd never guess this canyon was up here unless you already knew it."

He's right. Just in front of us two ridges meet like folded arms, and it takes a keen eye to see the passage that darts between them. It's so narrow that the Toyota brushes against the steeply rising walls. Rocks jut a foot out of the ground. Bret slams the steering wheel right, then left as the engine grinds against the grade.

"Don't have much need for fancy cars out here," he says. "Course, it don't help that we travel around on half bare tires, but we might as well get all the use out of them we can. Now . . . look."

We've come to the mouth of another canyon, invisible until this moment, though perhaps "giant natural amphitheater" better describes the formation. Rocky walls rise thirty stories tall on three sides from a jagged, boulder-strewn floor that stretches half a mile or so wide and twice that in length. The canyon floor is streaked with flash flood washes that cut through fields of sage. Juniper trees cling to life in small clumps, every branch bent low to the ground as if survival depends on it.

I swallow hard. I wanted remote but somehow I hadn't imagined a place so barren. Or perhaps it's just that I hadn't imagined *me* in a place so barren.

The wheel tracks are gone, and no semblance of a designated passageway remains.

Bret coaxes the Toyota up and over into a wash, a miniature flat-bottomed canyon much deeper than first appearance suggests. Up and over the next wash and then another, Bret jams the clutch to the floorboard, then pops it, sending the Toyota into involuntary but effective lurches. A deafening scrape underneath us brings Bret's hand to the emergency brake. "That's as far as she'll make it," he says.

I scramble out of the truck and zip my leather jacket against the wind. "Does it always blow this hard?"

"Updraft," Bret nods. "Can't avoid it in a canyon. If a real wind kicks up, and it may, you'll know it. Wind's one of the prime characteristics of a desert. We only get about five inches of rain a year to begin with, and most of that is evaporated by the heat and the wind. Twenty-five-thousand years ago the Great Salt Lake Desert was under water—an inland freshwater sea, known as Lake Bonneville, that covered parts of Nevada and Idaho as well as Utah. As the lake evaporated, saline concentrated in both the standing water and the exposed land. The Bonneville Salt Flats, a few hundred miles to the north, and the Great Salt Lake are both remnants of the giant prehistoric lake."

Shielding my eyes from the noontime sun, I look north beyond the amphitheater upon the vast desert floor, two thousand feet below. As far as I'm concerned, it still looks prehistoric. It's nearly solid white from saline in the soil, as smooth as the sea that once covered it. Even as I watch, the earth's crust is slowly, inexorably, pulling apart beneath my feet. The sea will return.

🐾

As a child, whenever my family camped, the campsite selection was the most crucial element. The process might take five minutes or an hour depending on the size of the campground and the number of occupants. We all knew that our choice set in motion the success or failure of our adventure. First, we drove through the campground pausing at each and every unoccupied site to evaluate its privacy, usually ensured by trees. Close to a water spigot but not too close that we would be bothered by other campers. Within walking range but not within smelling range of the toilets and garbage cans. Level and soft spots for however many tents we'd brought along, anywhere from one to four. As far away as humanly possible from campers who had brought radios or televisions. We considered those devices the ultimate insult to the camping experience, and we were embarrassed for anyone who didn't realize their offense.

None of those criteria play a role in the selection of the site I'll call my own for the next forty days. After briefly scouting the area, I settle on a spot at the base of the eastern wall. Not in a wash but in a type of basin, lower than the surrounding area, for I wish to be as discreet as possible. A clump of junipers will help shield the wind. A giant rock column at least four stories tall leans precariously outward from the sheer rock of the eastern wall. I imagine the Leaning Tower of Pisa stuck on the side of the cliff about a hundred yards above my head, because that's exactly what it looks like both in size and stability.

"Been here a million years," Bret shakes his head when I point it out. "Probably be here a million more."

A half hour later, my supplies are a small jumbled mountain stashed under a juniper tree. I pitch my tent, a red two-person dome, while Bret and Dana gather wood and dead sage for a fire.

"Right now you'll find plenty of dry branches on the ground," Bret says, "but one good snow would bury all that."

"Snow?" I finish driving a tent stake into the hard desert dirt and look at the ranger. "I thought it didn't snow until January."

"Shouldn't much," Bret agrees. "It's not unusual to get a good flurry before Christmas, but I wouldn't worry."

"Got my leather jacket," I say, "and ski pants. I'll be fine."

"I'd go crazy out here," Dana says. "At least I can watch television at my place and I'm still bored."

"I brought four blank journals and a few craft supplies," I say. "Paint, mostly, and a block of clay. If I get too restless, I can always make a pot." I've intentionally left most forms of entertainment behind in order to leave society itself behind. Not that I've ever tried it, but I suspect a mind diverted by the pleasant occupation of reading could easily forget its isolation. I've come here to be alone. I've come here to experience what the desert might contain. I won't, I can't, offer myself escape.

"Not even a book?" Dana asks, scrunching her nose.

"Just a desert guide." I don't mention the copy of *Walden Pond,* its cover nearly worn off, tucked inside my sleeping bag. I've read it so many times that I no longer count it as entertainment.

"I'd go *nuts,*" Dana repeats, "but I'm sure you know what you're doing."

No, I really don't, but it's starting to sink in.

"I guess this is it for us," Bret says, picking up his shovel. "You better keep this."

"I can't thank you enough for . . ." My words stop in my throat as I hear a strange sound like the rushing of a waterfall. It starts as a subtle whine high in the canyon walls, then becomes louder as if coming toward us. It is coming and then—*whoosh*—

it hits like a tidal wave. Dana grabs Bret to keep standing, and I'm practically lifted off my feet. And then it's gone.

"What the . . . "

"I told you you'd know it if the wind came up," Bret says.

"Wind? That's enough to make you think the world's coming to an end." I'm half joking, but Bret's face is serious.

"The desert's a funny place," he says. "It can do strange things to your mind." His voice makes me uneasy. I search his eyes for some trace of humor, but I'm not reassured. It's beginning to dawn on me that within minutes, I will be left here *alone*.

"Longest I ever stayed out was three weeks—me and another guy," Bret continues. "I'll never forget it. Being alone like you are, you'll be changed, there's no doubt about that. Remains to be seen whether that's for the better or the worse. The desert's a peculiar place. It's hard to keep your wits about you when it gets sticky— and chances are good it'll get sticky. If you get in a bind, try to remember: *one spot.* That's the key. Long as you got one spot where you feel safe, you'll make it."

I'm not sure what that means, but I nod. "I'm mostly worried about mountain lions. How likely is it any live around here?"

"Dad and I used to hunt 'em up in here before it got outlawed. Now that nobody's hunting, there's probably a bunch. Wouldn't worry, though. They're more scared of you than you are of them."

He doesn't know me very well or he'd realize that's impossible.

Bret guns the Toyota back to life and waves his arm out the window as if he were leaving a picnic on Sunday afternoon instead of stranding a woman in the desert.

"Bye, everybody!"

"Bye-bye!"

"See you next time!"

The truck lurches forward and my stomach lurches at the same time.

Alone.

Chapter Four

I am left in the most absolute silence I have ever heard, a silence so overwhelming that I understand within three seconds how the absence of sound could be called deafening. For several long moments I strain my ears for the rumble of the Toyota's engine, unwilling to accept that I can't hear it any more. Bret could have changed his mind about his shovel. Surely they'll be back in a minute. I stand on my tiptoes for the first glimpse, but after what seems like an eternity I realize they're really not coming back.

And so I am really alone.

I turn toward Pisa Rock without moving my feet. It's still there, but it seems to me that only by a stroke of dumb luck is it barely anchored to the cliffs. I swivel toward the mouth of the canyon. The view is unbroken for miles, all the way to the mountains in the west, and there is nothing between me and there. Nothing.

I feel as if I've fallen through a tunnel into another time. Back in grade school my sisters and I used to rush home to watch *Land of the Lost* on television. That's what had happened to them—a dad and his two kids fell through a tunnel and got trapped in prehistoric time. My sisters and I watched from the safety of our couch, munching peanut butter and banana sandwiches and sipping Kool-Aid as the father and his children managed one narrow escape after another from the ferocious dinosaurs. In those days we found the scenario entirely credible, but in this desert canyon I'm able to imagine the terrorizing scream of a Tyrannosaurus rex with an even better degree of accuracy.

My knees are actually shaking.

Why are there no birds? The silence is unnatural. Nothing could be this quiet unless it were trying to be quiet. Everything is hiding. The creatures of the desert must be all around me, lurking in the rocks and the sage and the cliffs. I feel their eyes boring into me, telling me I don't belong. I know that. Everything is still because everything is holding its breath waiting for me to be the first to break the silence, and when I do the air will burst with the screams of the mountain lions and the shrieks of the eagles and the roar of rocks tumbling down to smash me into pieces and the dinosaurs booming across the canyon . . .

I stop myself in mid-thought. This is ridiculous. It's not as if I haven't been alone before.

I have almost no specific memories of what happened the first month after leaving Denver. Perhaps the mind enfolds itself around events that are simply too painful to remember, dragging them deep into the subconsciousness like a shark with its teeth buried into a seal's neck, refusing to let them surface where they could possibly get loose. Most of that month is a blur, except for the moment I returned to California and knocked on the door of the house that for nine years I had called home.

I hadn't seen Tony in six weeks, and yet as he tumbled into my arms and I kissed him all over he pulled away and asked, "Why did you knock, Mommy?" I looked over his head to find Gina staring at me, trying to blink back the tears of a fourteen-year-old broken heart. James had already told her about the divorce, but we had agreed that I would be the one to tell Tony.

I led him out to the garden—that's what we still called it—but as I now took it in for what it had become, I realized that the outward signs of my marriage's decay had been more obvious than I'd allowed myself to see. When we first moved to the house the garden had been a little piece of paradise. The previous owners had built planter boxes, installed individual sprinklers and tiled the entire area with brick. They'd grown flowers, vegetables, avocados and lemons, but the rich soil had long since turned to sand. The planters were a mass of weeds and the trees drooped half to the ground: that is what apathy does to paradise.

I remember hoisting Tony onto my lap that afternoon, and I remember feeling the warm California sun on my shoulders. I remember the faint sound of the waves crashing onto shore a mile away and I remember the train that whistled somewhere in the distance. I remember that I pulled my son close and looked directly into his eyes, and I remember that his eyes got bigger and bigger and an expression of absolute horror gradually transformed his features until all at once he began to sob, his entire body shaking until my shirt was soaked.

But I don't remember a word I said.

Tony and Gina spent the night with me at a Motel 6. They swam in the pool and we ate at the adjoining Denny's restaurant.

The next day I took Tony to a baby-sitter and Gina went to a friend's house. I didn't want them to be home while I packed up my things.

The arrangements for my withdrawal, as the process most closely resembled, had been made with virtually no argument. It was almost as if James and I had always known that sooner or later this moment would come, and each of us had always known that I would be the one to do the deed. We didn't fight over the house. He would keep it. We didn't fight over the children. He would keep them during the school year and they would spend their holidays and summers with their respective mothers. We didn't fight over money or who was right or wrong.

Our only real argument erupted over Jerry.

"You can't tell me he didn't have anything to do with this," James said.

"I told you. We had dinner. He went back to Alabama. I thought I'd never hear from him again."

"But you did."

"Yes, but after I decided to call you. After I *had* called you."

"I suppose you think you're in love."

"God, James, I've only known him two weeks," I said. "He's just a friend."

That's what Jerry had said when he called my Denver dorm room just days before my departure. His timing was perfect. When I returned from getting my hair cut that afternoon the phone had been ringing.

"Just wanted you to know," said the voice belonging to the sea-green eyes, "if you ever need someone to talk to, you can count on me."

My words spilled into the receiver like water bursting from a dam. Jerry listened without interrupting for nearly an hour until the eruption had run its course.

"What're you going to do now?" he asked.

"I haven't gotten that far," I admitted. "I haven't even told my son yet."

"I'd invite you here, but it sounds like you need some time alone."

I took it. After talking to Tony, I drove into the Sierra Nevada and rented a one-room cabin for two weeks. It was time to listen to my soul.

Here in the desert, the silence is almost overwhelming. The emptiness is worse. I force my feet a few steps forward. I think I know how a bear feels, a naughty bear that's prowled in one too many campground garbage bins, and the rangers finally decide they've had enough. The last thing the bear remembers is a sharp pain in his butt, and when he wakes up he's in a place he doesn't recognize at all. He wanders around half-dazed, looking for any sign of familiarity. After a while he figures out that there's no hope. His instincts kick in, compelling him to establish a new territory right where he is.

I too feel that drive.

By means I don't quite understand, my eyes perceive the exact boundaries of my claim. On the north side, my red dome tent. On the south, the clump of junipers where my supplies are stored. On the east, the sheer wall of the cliff where Pisa Rock clings for its life. On the west, the subtle rise of ground bordering a wash on the other side. Perhaps altogether the space is thirty feet square, and I am aware that I would defend that space if I had to, to my death.

Until I can build the shelter, the tent is my den. I blow up the mattress, put it inside and arrange the sleeping bags atop it. As for everything else—the box of hardware and craft supplies, the box of propane canisters, my clothes and toiletries, the frying pan, coffeepot, newspapers for starting fires—I shove it all in the tent as well. There's no room for the canvas tarps and lumber, so I leave them beneath the juniper with the water jugs.

As dusk approaches, the white sands of the desert floor far below my canyon tinge blue by shadows that stretch for miles, cast from the high mountains to the west. The sun slips closer to the horizon and the cliffs glow peachy-brown, turning to dull gray as the sun dips behind the mountains. I wish I knew what time it was because surely the sun is late going down. In November it sets by 5:00 p.m., but I can't have been here only four hours. It feels like forever—and what will I do when the sun goes away?

Forcing the fear from my mind, I concentrate on setting a pot of water to boil on the propane stove. I can't help but wonder if I was unwise to limit myself to a diet of chickpea lentils and rice—simplicity in place of outright denial. Requiring only one pot for preparation, they provide a good balance of protein and carbohydrates. I've been a vegetarian for nearly three years, so I won't miss meat and I'll take a vitamin supplement. I wasn't going to bring coffee, flour, oil or salt, but some inner part of me must have known better. At the last minute I even packed a can of pumpkin and a can of olives for my Thanksgiving dinner.

I've stored all the food in a Coleman cooler to protect it from animals. Even as I open it, I remember the mouse that startled me at the grocery store. I open the lid slowly, as if by some chance the mouse stowed away, but all I find are neat rows of Ziploc bags filled with rice and chickpea lentils.

As the water heats, I toss the last of the wood Bret and Dana gathered for me onto the fire. It won't last long. Maybe I've watched too many movies where the natives fight off the tigers with blazing torches or where the lost hiker huddles near his campfire as the lion's yellow eyes glow in the shadows, but at this moment I believe all of it. Fire is my only weapon against the night, not to mention against the chill that is beginning to descend upon the canyon with surprising speed. I head off to collect more wood.

By the time I return with one armload—Bret was right, there's wood scattered liberally on the ground—the water is steaming. By the time I return with the third load, my ears are met with a sound so startlingly loud that it takes me several moments to identify it as the water boiling. Steam gushes into the air and with it rises the memory of all those cars I saw along the interstate in the Mojave, their hoods raised, owners hurrying to the call boxes. There are no call boxes here, and neither is it 105 degrees. Bret warned me of the desert's cold winter nights, but somehow the *idea* of forty degrees wasn't as cold as the reality now actually feels.

Pisa Rock has melted with the dusk to become one with the cliffs, and I toss a few more pieces of wood on the fire before sitting down as close to it as I can with my concoction of chickpea lentils and rice. There's something about the outdoors that makes even the most ordinary food taste better. On Girl Scout overnights as a child we used to make Brownie Stew, so named because even the youngest Brownie scout could prepare it: a couple of pounds of browned ground beef and a couple of cans of undiluted vegetable soup mixed together and heated in a pot. Feast fit for kings, we thought.

Between bites of my chickpea mixture—far nuttier and more

tasty than I had imagined possible—I scan the canyon for any movement. The cliffs seem to loom even higher and more solid, reminding me again how easily a falling rock could crush my head into pieces. In my Girl Scout days thoughts like this didn't disturb my appetite, but now I push my bowl aside.

The moon begins to peek into the canyon, drenching the cliffs in a silver hue. Pisa Rock emerges from the darkness, a gigantic phallus erect against a pelvis of stone. Perhaps the desert is already doing something to my mind, for my imagination runs wild with explanations for the formation's existence—explanations that would never appear in a textbook back in the world I left just this morning. I imagine that the giant stone is the remnant of an ancient evil giant who once pursued a beautiful maiden across this very desert. Just as he grabbed her hair, she turned to face him, no longer a beautiful maiden but instead the ugliest witch he had ever seen. He released her, but too late. Witches always win. With one mighty punch she knocked him flat on his back. The giant's phallus, frozen in time for at least another million years, is proof of his ill-fated pursuit.

As a child, witches with weirdly long noses terrified me in my dreams, cackling and flying through the heavens silhouetted against the moon. I dreaded sleep, convinced that the witches were real. Every few nights I'd show up in my parents' bed after encountering yet another witch in my dreams.

"Next time you see one," Mom said when I crawled in for the third night in a row, "tell her she's just a dream and she has to go away." I tried, but the witch just laughed at me. A few years later the nightmares finally ran their course, but sometimes I'm still uncomfortable looking at the sky, unable to completely forget them.

I toss another branch on the campfire, and flames leap toward the sky in a shower of sparks. A folded newspaper serves as my chair, and the cold seeps from the ground into my pants like ice water. I pull my leather jacket tighter around my chest as memories of other campfires play across my mind: laughing faces, voices raised in song, celebrations. I see my dad carry a load of wood from our garage into our living room in the heart of winter. I see my mom demonstrate how to carve a fire starter from a cedar twig to my Girl Scout troop. And then the memories fade as if to remind me that they are indeed only memories, not the same as the fire I sit before now.

I tip my head back at the moon. The broad band of dense stars stretching from one horizon to the other is the Milky Way. Beyond that the cosmos opens to infinite galaxies. I have never seen the sky so full of twinkling lights, not even in Alabama, where the fireflies flutter like dancing stars in rhythm to the songs of the crickets and the tree frogs.

After two weeks in the one-room cabin I had rented after telling Tony of the divorce and packing my belongings, I understood why Thoreau retreated to the woods for two years. In fourteen days I hadn't even come close to knowing what I wanted to do with the rest of my life. But I did have more insight into why it was easier to listen to my soul as a teenager. As a teenager I didn't have to worry about bills.

My household income had now dropped from sixty thousand dollars a year to almost nothing. No matter what my soul desired about avoiding humdrum routine, I would have to get a job to be able to afford an apartment. Freelance editing would never pay the rent and no matter what my soul said about having a unique purpose, and despite a college degree, I wasn't qualified for much of anything else. I would have to work as a store clerk—or some version thereof—and advance in a couple of years to management and a decent salary with benefits. Eventually. *Then* I could do whatever my soul desired.

The problem was that I just couldn't convince myself that there wasn't some other option. Surely adulthood didn't have to mean total immersion into tedium. Surely life could be more than working to pay off the credit cards from last summer's two-week vacation. I knew it could, because I had met a man who had managed to achieve it. So I turned to his counsel. After two weeks in the Sierras I packed my car again and drove to Alabama.

"You'll never catch it," Jerry said, watching me from the cottage porch as I tried to cup a firefly in my hands. I couldn't resist the challenge. I'd never seen the flashing bugs before, and I found them as magical as everything else about this cottage in the southern Appalachians.

The pictures hadn't nearly done it justice. They didn't show the ladder leading to the second-story sleeping loft where lace hung in soft folds from the ceiling, or the coffee table made from the bin of an old grist mill, or the antique furniture, or the Persian puppets and the arrowhead collection, or the fireplace and hearth made of stones from Jerry's grandfather's homeplace. I had never realized that four walls could contain not only a room but also a personality, for the cottage that began as a tree house seemed the physical manifestation of the soul belonging to the man who had walked nine hundred miles.

I had never felt so drawn toward another human being. In Jerry I saw what I wanted to be. In his life I saw what I wanted from mine. The purpose and meaning I had imagined for myself seemed to lurk just beyond my vision, just around the next bend.

"You'll figure it out," Jerry said. "Just don't box yourself in. It's easier to get a job and an apartment than to get out of them. Give yourself a little more time."

So I did. I camped and stayed at youth hostels and inexpensive motels, and my credit card balance shot skyward. That summer I worked as a cook at a camp for kids. The salary didn't make a dent in my debt, but at least Tony and I had a cabin to ourselves. I spent the next Thanksgiving in a hotel room with Tony, Christmas in Alabama with Jerry, and New Year's Eve with Tony in another hotel room. I spent Valentine's Day in Alabama and Easter in California. In between I managed to see most of the United States—more than once. I often detoured hundreds of miles out of my way because I really had no place else to go.

"Why did you and Dad have to get adopted?" Tony asked as I strapped him into his monster costume for trick-or-treating that Halloween.

"Divorced," Gina gently corrected.

"Yeah that," Tony nodded. "How come I can't visit you at your house?"

"Because I don't have one yet, honey."

"When are you gonna get one?"

The question weighed heavier as each day passed, and still I had not unraveled the mysteries of my soul. I still didn't know what to do with my life, and I didn't know where else to look for answers. I didn't know how much higher I could run up my credit cards. I didn't know how much longer I could bear living out of my car.

"I can't stand the thought of leaving," I told Jerry as I packed

Betsy for yet another early morning departure from Alabama.

"Then stay." He touched his fingers to my cheek as he had that first night at dinner in Denver. "I've always wanted the cottage to be more than a retreat. Even years ago when it was just a tree house, I hoped a woman would come along who could love it like I do. You were right. She was out there."

"I can't afford—"

"I'll back you until you get on your feet."

I thought of Tony. "I can't . . ."

"He can come here on his vacations. That's the great thing about cabins. Anytime you need space you just build another room. I'll build us a bedroom and Tony can sleep in the loft. I can have it done by Christmas."

Within weeks the new room began to take shape, and when Tony came at Christmas his eyes sparkled like tinsel.

"This is your *house?*" he laughed, scrambling up the ladder to his loft.

Somewhere in a distant corner of my mind, though, I realized that it really wasn't. The place was Jerry's, and this wasn't really my life. I still hadn't answered my questions. I still didn't know what to do for money. But as I watched the two most important people in my life unwrap their presents by a glowing fire in the hearth, I told myself that maybe I had found my answers without even knowing it. Maybe everything had taken care of itself, because I had never known happiness so complete.

A sudden gust of wind whipping through the desert canyon jolts me back to the present, as a sprinkling of rain splatters my bandanna. Rain? It's only a few drops, but they signal the end of my campfire. I flip on the flashlight to shine my path to bed. As I unzip the tent flap, I turn my eyes once more toward the moon, but clouds now streak the sky to mostly obscure its light.

The tent is crowded with my supplies, and the flashlight splashes their shadows against the nylon walls. I've slept in this tent a dozen times or more, but tonight it seems flimsy, offering no protection whatsoever against whatever might be *out there*. Maybe Bret was right. Maybe it isn't safe to venture into the wilderness unarmed. But what would I shoot? The air? How would I shoot my fears?

I've tucked one sleeping bag inside the other for extra warmth. I crawl inside, still dressed, and flip off the light. The phantoms on the walls are now even more ghostly, undulating in the flames from the campfire, the pattering of raindrops providing the percussion to their dance. I turn on the light again, knowing that sleep will elude me, and I open a blank journal. My hand trembles slightly as I pick up my pen, hesitating before I touch it to the paper as if it is reluctant to bring up the past. I, too, hesitate to face it.

The trouble began when Jerry decided it was time to start another book. In the six months we had lived together, I had accompanied him to dozens of his lectures and book signings. I sat by his side and smiled as he talked to readers about his journeys, journeys that he had taken before we met, journeys that had nothing to do with me. At first I'd been able to put aside the sensation that every sidekick feels—the subtle feeling of diminishment, the slight awareness that you're not actually necessary in the moment at hand. I couldn't help but resent that the new book would condemn me to years more of the same role.

It wasn't long until I noticed a change. Whereas once Jerry and I had spent nearly every minute together, now he worked all day at his word processor. Even when he was with me, I sensed he was in another world. Whereas before I had been content cooking, gardening and writing in my journal for hours on end, I began to feel that really I did nothing. Nothing important.

"I can't give up my career just because you haven't found one," Jerry said when I complained about the hours I spent alone. "Maybe you should get a job."

"That's just great," I said. "All this time you've been telling me not to and now you say I should."

"I never said you should do nothing."

"Then let's look at the alternatives. There are a hundred sock mills in this county. I could spend eight hours a day pairing socks. I think I heard that the feed store is accepting applications, or maybe I could work at Wal-Mart. Humdrum. That's exactly what I've been trying to avoid."

"OK, OK," Jerry said. "Don't work. You're only hurting yourself."

"I would have been better off if I'd never come here. At least in California there are good jobs."

"You didn't want any of them, either."

I couldn't argue with that.

"Look," Jerry said. "This is just a difficult phase you're going through. What you're feeling is perfectly natural. You got married a year after high school before you decided what you wanted to do apart from being a wife. You graduated from college unsure of what you wanted to do apart from being a mother. You just need to figure out what you want to do with your own life."

"I know what I *don't* want," I said. "I don't want to go through the rest of my life feeling like your sidekick, and that's all there is for me here." I paused and took a deep breath. "I'm sorry. You mean the world to me. I don't know where I'd be if I hadn't met you. Maybe you're right. It's been three years and I still haven't found what I really want to do, so maybe I should just get a job and get on with it.

"But I just *can't*. I don't know what it is inside of me that won't let me give up, but ever since I can remember, I've believed that I'm meant for something more. You once told me that what I'm looking for does exist. Maybe it's still a matter of what I'm willing to do to find it. I just . . . I just don't think I can find it here. I don't think I can find it with you."

"You're leaving?" he asked.

I couldn't answer except to nod.

"Are you coming back?"

"I don't know."

Jerry wiped a bead of sweat from his brow. "What about Tony? How can you take this away from him? I waited all of my life to find you, and now you're just walking away."

"I love you, Jerry. That's not the problem."

"I love you, too. I love you so much that I'd rather you be happy somewhere else than be miserable here with me. Maybe you'll find what you're looking for, maybe you won't. Maybe you'll find someone else, and . . . and maybe I will, too."

I wanted to say that I was wrong, that I would stay, that somehow we would work things out. But there was really nothing to work out. Either I was right—and the life that my soul reflected in the mirror so many years ago could be real, or I was wrong.

I left Alabama because I couldn't believe I was wrong. I could not have paid a higher price for that belief, except for my very life.

❧

I finally set my journal aside and flip off the flashlight. As I wait for sleep, I think back to Wanda at the grocery store. *Sometimes we can only hear our answers, no matter where they come from, in a quiet place.*

This place is so quiet I may lose my mind.

While you're out there, try to remember that you're not alone.

Oh yes, I'm alone.

It's pitch black hours later when I struggle to wake. A noise like thunder pounds in my ears. I know exactly where I am and I also know that I'm freezing. I'm *wet*. I finally register the beating on the nylon above my head. It's raining. It's raining *hard*. I am *soaked*.

I grope for my flashlight. I turn it on and the tent glows red, my eyes squinting in the sudden light. The moan that follows comes from so deep inside me that for a moment I wonder if I'm someone else. The tent is no less than half an inch deep in water, some places as much as two inches. And then I hear it, far off at first like a moan, and then closer, the same type of rush that preceded the tidal wave of—

Whoosh!

The tent bends half over, and water sloshes across the floor like a flood sent to sweep me into a world farther away than I have ever been.

Chapter Five

When I emerge from the shadows of a listless sleep, the pounding rain has ceased. The scientists were way off base with their prediction that the sea would return to the desert millions of years from now. It's already happened, right in my tent.

During the night, aided only by the single beam of my flashlight, I could not hope to explain the mystery of the tide rising all around me. But now as I lay on my back staring at the red nylon above my head, it's clear that the water didn't come in through the roof. The rainfly is still attached. True, the rain came down in a torrent but I've camped in storms before without so much as a drop seeping in. Obviously, far more than a drop seeped in last night, though I'm still not clear how.

I scoot halfway out of my sleeping bags and meet the cold's sharp bite. I unzip the tent's door and poke my head out, face raised to the sky. The sun radiates silver-yellow beams against a pale blue sky. Not even a cloud lingers as evidence of the rain.

I can't dismiss the thought that the phenomenon of too much water has more than once been attributed to God's displeasure with the human race. That this particular flood appears to have been limited to my tent, and that I can't explain exactly how and where the seepage occurred, does nothing to boost my confidence. Neither does my second discovery of the morning: The one thing that should have protected me from the water—the air mattress I bought new specifically to ensure no leaks would condemn me to sleep on hard ground for forty nights—is thoroughly flat beneath me. I am sitting in the lake.

I'm dying for a cup of coffee, but the need for dry clothes is even more pressing. By some miracle my bag of clothes ended up on top of the cardboard box that holds the propane canisters, which disintegrates as I pull it toward me. I step outside to change into long underwear, leggings and a flannel shirt. My Reeboks float like two little boats within the tent. I rummage for the cowboy boots.

There is no choice but to completely empty the tent and mop it out. The sleeping bags leave a wake as I haul them to the makeshift shore. Separating the outer from the inner bag, I'm relieved to find that only the outer one is completely soaked. The inner bag is merely damp, except the bottom two feet. Maybe it's not overly optimistic to think they'll dry during the day. I spread them both atop the tent and drag the remaining boxes and bags outside.

"OK, who hid the towels?" I say aloud, digging into the closest box. The sound of a voice, even my own, raises my spirits. After all, a little rain never hurt anyone. Just a little bump in the road, that's all. Every journey has a glitch—it's to be expected—and now I've got the glitch out of the way. From here on out. . . .

Pushing aside a sweater and a flannel shirt, I spot the blue and white striped fabric of kitchen towels. They're all I brought in the wipe-up department. I knew I wouldn't be showering, and I didn't know I'd be mopping up a lake. I grab a corner of the towel and tug it from the box, trying not to pull everything else with it. Having retrieved only one, I dig back into the box, almost to the very bottom, and my hand touches something hard wrapped in something soft.

This time I don't grab a corner and pull. This time I empty the box and carefully raise the towel-enshrouded object to the surface. My fingers gently press back the cloth and a red face stares up at me. A life-size mask carved from a hollowed-out gourd split in half in the manner of Cherokee traditions hundreds of years old. Its mouth is an open and nearly perfect circle made even wider by rings of black and yellow and white. The rings match those around the open eyes. A yellow starburst flares across each red cheek and in the center of the forehead. Three strands of coarse twine two feet long hang from its chin. A single feather is the only headdress.

"To watch over you," Jerry had said as he placed the mask in my hands the morning I left Alabama. "I hope that when you find your answers, you will also find ours."

He never spoke a word against my decision to come to the desert, but my son was less encouraging. "Why, Mom?" Tony, now nine years old, asked when I told him of my plan. "You could *die.*"

And my parents. "Are you sure about this?" Dad said when I called him and Mom in Taiwan. He didn't say it, but I knew what he was thinking. This is the kid who's afraid of mice. This is the kid who's afraid of the stars. This is the kid who slept with us because she thought witches were real.

My eyes trace the thirty-foot-square boundary in the canyon that only last night I established as my territory, now littered with soggy supplies as if to hammer home how quickly reality as well as perception can change. I wouldn't want Jerry or Tony or my parents to see me now. What frightens me is that perhaps for the first time I see myself as they would, if they could.

After three cups of coffee I'm ready to face the rest of the day. Last night's lesson is that I need to build the canvas shelter as soon as possible. I don't want to be caught off guard again.

As the canyon floor is a continuous downhill slope, I'll have to level up a site for my shelter. I estimate the necessary plot as about eight feet square. The high end rises a foot above the low end. That's a lot of dirt to move just to make a flat sleeping surface. At least the ground is soft from the rain.

I ask a prayer of forgiveness as I dig up a sage bush. Twenty years of effort stopped dead in its tracks. I probably would have had to dig up some sage anyway, given that all the firewood on the ground is soaked. The sage takes to the flame immediately, and I'm surprised at the laugh that spills from my lips. "A-*ha*," I say, tossing the second sage into the fray, "a burning bush."

With my boxes and bags and Reeboks arranged around it, the fire provides more ammunition in the battle to dry out. Its crackles are pleasant company in the stillness, broken only by the sound of my borrowed shovel pressing into the dirt.

By the time the sun has passed halfway through the canyon— probably three hours or more—I'm sick of shoveling. My feet are freezing. The cowboy boots are now coated in mud, and my socks aren't thick enough to deflect the cold. Maybe that explains the boot stuck on the fence post yesterday. Maybe its owner discarded the piece of junk in the most convenient way at hand, because it is now more than obvious that cowboy boots are not the footwear of choice when it's been raining in the desert.

I take a break to sit by the fire, wishing again that I had brought a chair. The newspaper pile resists seepage for about four minutes, just long enough for the flames to heat the cowboy boots on my outstretched legs to the steaming point. A moment later the sole of the left boot curls back to reveal the toe of my green sock.

"Great," I murmur. "Just great."

Looking to improve my situation by at least some tiny degree, it occurs to me that to fit the lumber for the shelter into Betsy's trunk the hardware man cut off the ends of the two-by-fours, and I brought the remnants along. They're the perfect length to construct a director's chair—the kind with the criss-cross frame and a canvas seat and the star's name in big letters across the back. I guess this is the only way I'll ever get to be the star.

A quick check through the soaked box of hardware supplies produces the bag of nails. I only brought one size: big, maybe two and a half inches long.

My eyes know at once what needs to be done: cross two boards together and drive a nail through the intersection. My hands, however, are less accomplished than my eyes. *Twang,* the nail flies through the air. *Plunk,* I miss the nail and the boards fall apart. *Bang bang bang* so far so good, *bang bang bang. Thunk*—the nail bends in half. I start eight nails before successfully driving three. I'm not sure those three are enough, but that's the best I can do. A couple of crossbeams later I'm ready to introduce the frame to a canvas cover, which I'll tack on with staples. A second trip to the hardware box produces the staple gun—another of the few "new" items I bought.

Usually staple guns come with at least an initial supply of staples. This one didn't, so I purchased a box of staples separately. I open the box, slide a row of staples out, and push them into the base of the staple gun.

But they won't be pushed. They're wider than the staple gun's slot.

I'm doing something wrong, except I'm not. They don't fit. But they *have* to fit. The salesman said they were the right ones. They don't fit.

This isn't possible. I can get by without a chair, but I can't get by without staples. There's no other way to tack the canvas to the shelter's frame—once I manage to build it—the shelter I realize I need now more than ever. To use those huge nails, even if I could drive them in, would be like wrapping a Christmas present with thumbtacks. I've already seen enough evidence of the wind to know it would rip the canvas to shreds in minutes flat.

I am furious with the salesman's carelessness and with myself for trusting him. I don't know if I can live in a *tent* for thirty-nine more nights, especially one that leaks. My only option is to hike five miles to the bush Bret pointed out for emergency communication, but judging by the sun's position it's too late in the day to start a ten-mile hike anyway. As I scan the sky, I'm surprised to notice clouds above the mountain range to the west. They don't look like normal clouds—not that I'm any more of an expert on clouds than I am telling time by the sun. They seem darker than normal clouds; darker even than rain clouds. At first I simply find them a curiosity, but when I look again to check the sun's progress the clouds appear closer. And now the sun disappears. I don't think it's because the sun hastened its journey toward the horizon. I think it's because the clouds hastened their journey toward *me*.

They seem to be rushing straight toward my canyon, stampeding across the sky. Ten minutes ago the sun shone bright. Now I can't even see the sky, and it's getting colder by the second. My family rarely camped in alpine areas, but I hiked enough on the lower slopes of Mount Rainier in Washington to have learned that some mountains create their own weather. If the sky couldn't change on a dime, there would never be hikers lost in freak storms. It's now painfully clear that the desert isn't immune to the same effect.

The clouds proceed at breakneck speed to blot out the desert floor, two thousand feet below my canyon, picking up momentum as each instant passes. Cold, white mist rushes before them to fill the canyon with thick, white fog.

This isn't normal fog. It's too cold. I've got to get out of it. This isn't right. It isn't *right*.

I scramble to hoist the boxes of supplies back into the tent. I grab my wet sleeping bags, shove them inside and hardly zip the door behind me when the tent is slammed by a wind far fiercer than any last night. The rain follows instantly in a torrent, but then I realize the pounding on the nylon is too loud to be rain. I peep out the door and my nose is slapped by a hundred pellets of hail. Not even a flicker remains of the campfire.

Another gust whips the nylon. The rainfly blows like a bubble on the roof, held down at its corners by hooks tucked into loops. Last night the tent withstood the brutal wind. So far it's survived the hail, but I peer out the door to see that it's started snowing— not soft and gentle flakes but a swirling mass that obliterates the sky. This is every hiker's worst nightmare. I am trapped in a blizzard and there is no way to safety.

When in a sudden gust the rainfly is ripped from the tent, I understand that I am in deeper trouble than I have ever known before.

Chapter Six

After four hours I still don't dare venture outside, though I'm hardly more protected by my tent. Even the rainfly wasn't enough to keep two inches of water out last night, and now I'm without it. I *must* find the rainfly. It's my only protection against the snow. On more nights than I can remember, I purposely left it off while camping so I could stare through the nylon webbing at the stars. But that was when I camped in parks, surrounded by other campers. I thought then that I was alone. I didn't yet know what alone means. Now I know.

I must find the rainfly. I must go into the storm, insulated only by my leather jacket. It isn't enough, but it should have been enough. Even Bret Layman agreed.

My fingers fumble with the screen-door zipper, then the front flap. I scoot outside, flashlight in hand. Icy pellets slap my face. The wind forces my breath backward into my lungs, and I gasp for air. I shine the light but see nothing in the swirling mayhem of ice. It is hopeless. For all I know my rainfly became a kite, caught in an updraft to sail out across the desert. If only I had leaped after it, catching each corner in my hands to make it billow like a parachute, I could have escaped with it.

I return to the tent without the rainfly. I must give up. I'm so tired that I long for sleep. Now I know I'll never wake. I'm too cold. It hurts to breathe. I will be dead before morning. They will find my body, frozen solid, wrapped in the sleeping bag that should have kept me warm, entombed in the tent that should have kept me dry. The evening news will run a story. "A woman who was determined to spend forty days and forty nights alone in the Great Salt Lake Desert has been found dead. Rescue officials were unable to reach her during the freak storm that swept through the area Saturday night. Officials are still investigating, but speculate that the woman's rainfly tore off her tent when the winds raged upward of sixty miles an hour."

It is pitch dark, hours before the dawn that I won't live to see. I am too scared to be scared.

If only the wind would stop, I could try again to get the rainfly. But it's blowing stronger than ever now, howling louder. I can't go back into the storm. I *can't,* but I have to. I reach for my Reeboks, still soaked from last night's rain. Either they shrunk or my feet have swelled. I fear the latter. My feet are blocks of ice. I don't bother with the laces.

I kneel in front of the door, bracing myself for the icy pellets. My fingers grasp the zipper and pull. It won't budge. I wiggle the metal tongue. It won't come loose. The nylon walls billow wildly in the wind as if they are as frantic to be free. They whip around me, cackling like a witch at my struggle.

Adrenaline rushes through my veins, and I yank on the zipper with both hands. It gives a little and I yank again and then again. The zipper jerks halfway up, now caught in the fabric. I struggle on my stomach to squirm through the opening. Swirling ice slams across my cheeks as I push my flashlight through ahead of me and cover my eyes with my arm. The light reflects off the gyrating snow and diffuses into the darkness. My lungs burn with ice. The wind is determined to blow me off my feet, to pick me up like a rag doll, to hurl my body against the cliffs.

A dark, swaying figure looms before me, and I start to turn back just as my eyes register it as a juniper tree. Its branches bend nearly to the ground and then swing high above my head. One branch dangles as if it snapped and now hangs by a thread. It flutters wildly, like a flag waving on a pole. A bright red nylon flag. I finally realize it's the rainfly. Eight feet in the air, and now it touches the ground, and now it soars toward the sky.

It's about twenty-five feet to the tree and I force my legs forward, keeping my eyes on the juniper. I can't breathe. Mucus freezes solid in my nostrils. A gust of wind sends a new wave of swirling ice into my face. I panic as the tree disappears. I look behind me and the tent is gone, invisible through the snow. I push forward, blind.

The wind lulls for an instant and I see the tree before it again disappears, long enough to know I wandered too far left. I claw forward. I should have reached it by now. My leather jacket is coated in ice. I gasp for each breath. My feet burn. My face feels frozen. My whole body aches.

I almost cry out with relief when the wind dies for a moment and the tree is within reach of my fingers. I shine the light into the top branches and spot the rainfly. But it is too high. A gust of wind blows the rainfly toward me. I grab only a corner before another gust tears it loose in a cruel game of keep-away.

I shine the flashlight again into the limbs. Careful . . . careful . . . wait . . . wait . . . *now.* I manage to grab a corner, nothing more, but it will have to be enough. At the next gust I yank with all my might and the rainfly comes free.

I drop to my hands and knees, clutching the nylon in my teeth. The twenty-five feet to the tent is a mile. The wind rages and as I gulp for air the rainfly flies from my mouth. I tackle it to the ground, refusing to lose my grip.

The tent flaps in front of me like a hot-air balloon straining against its tether in a tornado. Only my supplies stored within keep it from sailing away. It is my only shelter, my only chance, and it is hardly better than nothing.

My gloves are too stiff to tie the knots necessary to reattach the rainfly. I peel one glove off, but my fingers hardly wriggle. I grip the flashlight between my elbows to free up my hands. Each corner must be tied down. One done. Two done. On the third the flashlight drops from my elbows. It dies as it hits the ground. I am in total darkness, alone in the desert. My God, what was I *thinking?*

I drop to the ground, fumbling gloveless for the light. I seize something hard and bring it close to my face but it's only a rock. My outstretched palms sweep in circles as I crawl forward finding nothing, nothing, and then my left hand touches something hard. Something long. My fingers search for a switch and the snow glows in a sudden puddle of light. I struggle to my feet and tuck the flashlight under my chin to shine on the two final knots, and at last I grope my way back through the half-zippered tent door.

The zipper refuses to budge, caught tight in the fabric. My

fingers are too numb to work it loose. I bend down and work it with my teeth. At last the zipper gives way and the snow is locked outside.

I tunnel into the sleeping bags, but I'm still freezing. I can't stop shaking. The wind blows so fiercely that it sounds like an avalanche. The rainfly billows like a parachute above the tent, and the next second it is ripped away.

It is gone. Ice falls freely onto my hat and cheeks.

I can't go back into the storm. I don't want to die.

For hours now the storm has pounded around me, on me, even through me, as if it has found a way to enter my bloodstream and seep into my bones. Without the rainfly I am lost, but I can't face the storm again.

I realize I have never known what cold really is, what cold really does. As a child, wading in the Puget Sound with my sisters, our feet first cried in pain before they got used to the water. It's not so bad, we told each other, once they're numb. But we never knew this kind of numb. Numb doesn't stop the pain. Numb doesn't stop the needles, like when the sleeping foot now wakes. Numb only transfers the agony from the skin into the marrow. The epidermis feels no trace of sensation, but each thread of tissue underneath begs to stop the torture.

The wind roars on and on. I must go after the rainfly, but I can't bring myself to face the wind again. I'm afraid of the wind. I don't know how to fight an enemy I can't see.

"One spot," I remember Bret said before he left me here alone. "As long as you've got one spot where you feel safe, you'll make it." I should have asked him what he meant. There is no *one spot*.

I am not safe. I'm not going to make it. My hands are ice cubes tucked under my armpits. I can move my fingers but I can't stop shivering, even with my leather jacket, even inside my sleeping bags.

A sudden explosion rings out above my head. The tent walls whip even more wildly than before.

I fear that I know what has happened, but there's only one way to find out. I scramble from my sleeping bags and push my swollen feet into the Reeboks, holding my breath as I touch the metal tongue of the zipper. It pulls easily now that my fingers have some sensation, but I worry that whatever feeling has been restored won't last long outside.

Pushing through the tent flap, I feel the wind land on me like a sumo wrestler and it knocks me to the ground. My cheek burns where it smashes on the fallen snow. I rise to my knees and crawl around to the side of the tent, holding the flashlight before me—one tiny flicker in a sea of swirling snow and darkness.

I lean close to the nylon walls, searching for the pencil-thin fiberglass tent poles. My fingers, already prickling, probe up the pole. The pole is comprised of a series of hollow rods with aluminum fittings at each joint, kept taut by an inner elastic cord. My fingers work past the first fitting and then the next. And then I feel it: The pole has snapped. I shine the light, gauging the damage. Only the cord prevents the pole from collapsing. If it weren't for the other pole, the tent itself would collapse.

I've got to find the rainfly, but I'm too afraid of the wind. I hobble around to the tent door and crawl inside, zipping the flap against the storm. I shine my light on the wall to trace the outline of the broken pole wondering how long it will hold.

I can't believe God brought me here just to let me die. But

no, this isn't God's fault. I'm the one who chose to come here. I'm the one who left Betsy behind. If only she were here I could crawl inside. I could start the engine and turn on the heater and be *warm.*

I tunnel under the sleeping bags. I must keep my head. I must get through the night. I promised Tony I'd be back in time for Christmas. I'll be back. I promised.

A second explosion rings out above my head as the second pole snaps. The tent implodes around me. Nylon slaps against my face. I can't breathe. I sit up, pushing my arms above my head with all my might. I must get air. I come to my knees, pushing the nylon up, up. Now *I* am the tent pole. Within minutes my shoulders ache. It's too cold, even colder than before. My outer sleeping bag is frozen solid. I'm exhausted.

I know about hypothermia. As the body chills from its 98.6 degree norm, changes begin to occur. At 97 degrees, the temperature control center in the hypothalamus alerts the surface-level capillaries, those tiny veins closest to the cold. *Constrict,* the capillaries are ordered, so the body's extremities—the hands and feet—begin to ache. Other muscles begin to tighten in preparation for what will occur at 95 degrees. The muscles having tightened now abruptly contract. The body trembles violently in a last-ditch effort to warm itself. Mild hypothermia has now set in. Judgment begins to fail. By 93 degrees, slight to moderate amnesia. 91 degrees, dull indifference. 90 degrees, total stupor. Without warmth, it's all downhill from there.

I am exhausted. I don't know what my body temperature is, nor how low it will go.

"Nice teeth," they'll say when they find my body. "Nice and clean. Straight, too."

"What a shame that a woman with such pretty teeth would die so young," they'll say. "She must have worn braces."

I did, but I won't be alive to tell them. My arms aren't strong enough to control a tent that has sprouted wings, a sparrow lost at sea in the middle of a hurricane. The wind is too strong for me. The cold is too much for me. If I could only close my eyes, just for a moment. . . .

Images spin and I am riding a carousel on a shiny blue horse. Round and round we go: faster, faster. Round and round: *faster, faster.* I am five years old, flying through the air, the wind blowing in my hair. I feel so free, so good, so *alive,* so free, and then the blue horse disappears beneath me and I am flying.

And now I see my daddy and I jump into his arms. I throw my arms around his neck, and he twirls me in the air. I see his face, and then I see my son. Then I'm the one on the ground and he's the one in the air. His arms wrap tight around my neck as I twirl him faster and faster. He laughs and laughs and then it isn't his laugh I hear, but Jerry's. I take Jerry's hand and we run through the forest, jumping over stumps, laughing. I feel so free, so good, so alive, so free.

But then the forest becomes dark. I spin around, but Jerry is gone. The stumps begin to grow into gigantic rocks that tower over my head so tall that I can't see where they end. They grow wider as they surge toward the sky. I try to run, but my legs are lead. The stones crowd closer, trapping me within a circle. I feel their weight on my chest and arms, squeezing all the air, all the life, out of me. I can't breathe.

I did not come here to die. I will not give up—that is not who I am. I am a fighter. I will fight. But it is too late. I am dead.

Chapter Seven

I don't know where I am when I open my eyes, not to darkness but to a faint shimmer of light. I struggle to make sense of the freezing weight that crushes my body. The weight is awful. The last thing I remember is the rocks, strangling me in their vise, and then I remember that I am dead. But I can't be dead. Death couldn't hurt this much.

I'm buried under snow. It hurts to be buried. I can't remember if I've ever been buried before. I think Tony wanted to bury me in the sand one day at the beach, but I wouldn't let him. Or maybe I wanted to bury him and he wouldn't let me. Or maybe he did let me. All my memories are fuzzy.

Slowly I remember. Sometime in the night my arms gave out and I couldn't hold the tent above me any longer. I don't know when the wind began to settle. I don't know when the snow stopped falling, only that it buried me before it did, determined to complete its mission.

I rise to my knees and snow slides off the tent above me. I fumble for the zipper on the front flap and crawl outside on my stomach. My eyes squint in the brilliant light as if they've forgotten how to see. At first there's only white. No shapes, no shadows, nothing but white so bright that it really isn't white but gold and silver and iridescent violet and stars shooting straight at me all mixed together.

I stumble to my feet and forms gradually begin to emerge, slowly melding into more distinct shapes. Shadowy blobs transform into juniper trees sparkling with ice; gray knee-high mounds metamorphose into tangled, snow-tinted sage. Barrel-sized rocks jut out of the ground like icebergs floating on a frigid sea.

Every muscle in my body aches. My mouth tastes like mold. My hands are on fire as I dig through the snow near the juniper where my water is stored. All sixty-three remaining gallons are frozen solid. I grasp two of the shorter two-by-fours, the type from which I constructed the director's chair frame. I drag them back to the tent, crawl inside, and prop the boards against the tent walls. It's not much of a shelter, but at least I am no longer the tent pole. I collapse atop my sleeping bags, my breaths short and fast, pillows of mist in the air.

If only I could brush my teeth and make them stop chattering. I can't stand the taste in my mouth but even if I could remember where I put the toothbrush, there's only ice to brush them with. Everything soaked by the rain is now frozen—including the dishtowels, including my clothes, shoes, gloves and knit cap.

I'm shivering all over, and I'm afraid my feet may be frostbitten. I have to warm up, I've got to have coffee but the water's frozen in the pot. It will melt if only I can remember where I put the matches. I find them in a Ziploc bag, and there's the tooth-brush, in the same baggy. My fingers are so numb it takes three tries to strike a match, but the burner finally catches a spark and flickers to life. I rub my hands over the flame but hardly feel the warmth. The burner is nothing next to the cold. I light the other burner and set the coffeepot atop it and then light the lantern—anything for heat—but it's not enough. Only a fire can give that warmth. A fire or warm, dry blankets. Both are equal impossibilities.

Surely Bret and Dana have notified the authorities. All I have to do is wait. I'm in no shape to walk five miles out of here, nor could I survive a night if I stumbled into a snowdrift, unable to find the road. But if they don't come soon I fear I will freeze as solid as the water jugs. No matter what it takes I must have a fire. No matter what it takes I must find dry wood.

My feet are so swollen that they hardly squeeze into the Reeboks, or perhaps the shoes are frozen rigid, I'm not sure. Even frozen they're the better option than the cowboy boots, whose smooth soles slip in the snow. My feet cry out with every step as I head up the canyon wall toward Pisa Rock. Four dead junipers stand out against the snow like scarecrows. They'll burn, if I can get to them.

The higher I climb the slope toward the junipers, the smaller and flatter the heap of red nylon below me appears. My body could have been lying inside it, all life gone, and for a moment a strange sensation comes over me that it actually is. My body is beneath the nylon, useless and dead, and I am far above it, peer-ing at what I once was. I picture what I look like, curled in the fetal position, for during those last minutes I found peace; my eyes closed, my fingers relaxed, my bangs like frozen hay across my forehead. I feel bad for her, the woman who died in the storm. And yet, it was time for her to go.

As I stare into the canyon where she took her final breaths, I am suddenly struck with a clarity I've never had before; an understanding that even now I can't truly understand, only perceive. Someday it won't matter how hard I fight. Someday I will die.

I stare at my fingers with the same urgency that I examined Tony's hands on the day of his birth, overcome by gratitude that all ten fingers functioned, awed by the creation of such tiny miracles in flesh. I lean my full weight into the branch of the first dead juniper, marveling that what no longer lives may still provide me with sustenance, just as dinosaurs long gone provide an entire world with oil. The branch hardly budges. I wrap my arms around it and lift my feet off the ground and bounce as hard as I can. I marvel that I'm alive to pitch my strength against that of a tree. When the branch at last snaps and I hoist it to my shoulder to drag back to camp, my lungs burn from exhaustion. But to me the pain is only a reminder that I can feel pain. I am alive to feel it.

By some stroke of fortune the bag of newspapers didn't get soaked by the rain, and those in the middle of the stack aren't frozen. I shake the snow off of a couple of dead sage bushes and they jump to life in the paper flames. As I hoped, the dead juniper limbs finally provide the warmth my body needs, though even with my feet practically on top of the fire they remain completely numb.

I don't understand why the rescue crew hasn't arrived. The sky is perfectly clear, perfectly silent. There should be no delay getting a helicopter into the area. And yet, as I scan the canyon wondering where the giant bird would land, it dawns on me that the actual signs of the blizzard are few. The deepest snow seems to have fallen within the thirty-foot-square territory I call my own—a fact I register in the same corner of my mind that noted the confinement of yesterday's flood to my tent; elsewhere only a scattering covers the ground, and the cliffs themselves are bare stone. Pisa Rock boasts hardly a dusting.

Bret and Dana live twenty-five miles away and at an elevation two thousand feet lower. It's possible the storm wasn't nearly as severe there. It's possible they have no clue that I need help. Given the lack of helicopter blades chopping through the canyon's silence, I have to say that it's even likely. Maybe I'm not going to be rescued. Maybe I'm going to have to save myself.

This reality sinks in slowly, partially because I have never had to consider what saving myself actually means. In third grade I memorized the elements essential to life just as I memorized the vowels of the alphabet: food, shelter, clothing, love, *a e i o u* and sometimes *y* and sometimes *w*. My teacher, Mrs. Darling, insisted upon the inclusion of *w* although I have never once come across an example of *w* acting as a vowel. She also insisted that *love* be considered an essential element of life because she said that was the one most difficult to live without.

Maybe she was right, but I suspect her theory was never tested by having to survive a night in the desert with only a collapsed tent for a shelter. I also suspect she never had to build an improved version out of lumber and canvas and two-inch-long nails.

My plan is to construct an A-frame with the two-by-fours, using the four-by-four for the center beam. I shovel the snow away from the area I began to level off yesterday. The sun now shines brightly, not enough to warm the air but enough to make very cold slush out of my leveling project. The slush is too much for my Reeboks, so I switch to the cowboy boots. Long before the ground is level, the sole of the right boot separates from the leather upper, matching the condition of the left. The freezing mud oozes between my toes and I chide myself for skimping in the foot-protection department. I should have known better. I did know better. Good shoes aren't cheating.

By the time the sun is midway across the sky, I've built the frame. It looks like a miniature swing set without the swings. If I were ever to gift wrap a swing set I might follow the same proce-dure I now employ to cover the frame with canvas. I spread the canvas on the ground, lift the frame onto my shoulder—I can barely manage the weight—set it atop the canvas, and pull the canvas up and over the center beam.

As I feared, the nails are simply too big, and the canvas rips where I drive them in. When the wind blows the canvas flaps so hard it looks like a wild turkey trying to take flight. I don't know how long it'll stay together. The other problem is the door. With the one remaining tarp I fashion a triangle about the size of the front opening and nail the tip and the upper sides to the frame. It too flutters in the breeze, and I wonder how it would have fared during last night's blizzard. I can guess.

In fact, as I examine the completed shelter I can't help but wonder if I've improved my circumstances at all. My shelter re-minds me vaguely of pictures I've seen of Gosiute Indian dwell-ings. When the early White Man crossed the Rockies to spill onto the Great Salt Lake desert, they encountered the Gosiute scat-tered throughout the region in small family groups. The Gosiute built simple huts called wickiups, limbs bound in a teepee ar-rangement but shorter and—without the availability of buffalo or deer hide—covered only with brush. The White Man pronounced them the poorest and most wretched of all North American Indians.

I sit on a stack of folded newspapers, watching the flames of my campfire, knowing that ancient dwellers in this same desert once gathered around their own life-giving force. My third grade teacher never mentioned *fire* as an essential element. Perhaps that's because outside the desert the meaning of fire has evolved since ancient time. Even in third grade I knew that to flick a switch meant instant heat—no need to gather around the flames. My mom cooked with the flip of a dial without needing to preciously guard the coals for the next day's meal. My family enjoyed an occasional fire in the fireplace. We even purchased split wood each fall delivered by a man in a flatbed truck—oh, how I complained about having to help Dad stack it in the garage—but I never fully understood that the enjoyment of fire was a luxury unknown until modern time.

As the flames grow stronger, they begin to draw moisture from the wet wood. Tiny bubbles first form and then burst to evaporate into the smoke, hissing a soft song that sounds strangely like *hello. Hello,* it seems to whisper, *hellooo,* and I understand why ancient peoples believed that a spirit dwells deep within the fire's center.

Hellooo . . .

Will my ears ever adjust to the desert's stillness? And yet, I'm not imagining that sound. It *sounds* like hello. It *sounds* like human voices. In the fire. *Helloooo.* It's louder now.

I jump to my feet. It's not my imagination, it couldn't be. I run to the top of a wash and peer down toward the mouth of the canyon. I see nothing—nothing except junipers and sage and rocks—but again I hear an unmistakable *hellooo.*

I turn all around, scanning the canyon walls. The wind—it

must be the wind. But the wind is calm; even the nylon tent is still. *Hellooo,* I hear again. It isn't the wind. It isn't the fire.

The sun, now partially eclipsed behind the high western mountains, casts long, broad strokes of yellow across the darkening sky to scatter the canyon in shadows. I shield my eyes and strain to discern sagebrush from rocks. There, those two, down the canyon, those two sage bushes. One's taller than the other. I can't remember if they were there before. I can't tell if they're moving. They are—or maybe they aren't—I can't tell.

Helloooo . . . anybody there?

And now the sage bushes come closer and I see that they're actually two bundles of coats and scarves and hats. The voice suddenly becomes clear. "Are you all right?" The shorter one unwinds a scarf to reveal Dana's anxious face. "We didn't know. The storm was bad at the house. We didn't know if you'd be . . ."

"Got here soon as we could," Bret says, unwrapping his scarf. "The truck wouldn't make it through the snow. We walked the last two miles. Sure am glad to find you in one piece."

"I told you we should have called for help." Dana shakes her head before turning to me. "He said we could get here just as quick . . ."

"I said you wouldn't want me to call in the cavalry unless it was absolutely necessary," Bret says, but the doubt is clear in his eyes.

I have to fight to hold back the tears that have without warning sprung to my own. "My tent poles busted in the wind. First one, then the other. I held it up all night."

"My God," Dana breathes. "You could've . . ."

"All the water jugs are blocks of ice," I say. "My sleeping bags are wet, my boots are leaking, my feet are numb, but I built a shelter today. It's the best I could do because I brought the wrong staples, but maybe it'll hold together as long as there's not another storm."

"You're not seriously thinking of . . ." Dana says, looking at Bret in unspoken agreement. Bret silently circles the shelter, and for the first time I realize that my site looks like a scene out of *The Three Little Pigs.* In one corner the heap that used to be my tent is the first little pig's house of straw, blown all to pieces when the big bad wolf went to huffing and puffing. In the other corner is my new shelter, the second little pig's effort: tan canvas slung over a shaky frame. The house made of bricks remains in the fairy tale.

"Look," Bret starts, turning to me, "I don't want to tell you your business, and it's not my decision to make. But I can't recommend you stay here. Nobody expected a blizzard this early in the season. I wouldn't feel right telling you it won't happen again, because it might. You're just not prepared for major weather."

"Why don't you come home with us," Dana offers. "At least for a night. Take a shower, long as you want. Warm up, sleep in a nice cozy bed, and decide in the morning if this is really what you want to do."

All I have to do is say the word. A two-mile hike to a warm truck, an hour's drive to a warm shower. I can leave the desert behind, the canvas shelter behind, the pile of nylon and broken poles—behind me, all of it—and go back.

Back to what?

For the second time today a strange sensation comes over me, and I once again feel as if I am somehow above the scene on the canyon floor. Once again I picture a woman lying dead among the folds of my tent. How strange it is to know her well. If the choice had been hers, she would leave the desert in a heartbeat.

After a long hot shower she'd call her parents from the wildlife refuge. "Mom? Dad? I couldn't do it. I had to give up." She could bring herself to say it because, after all, it is nothing new for her to give up. She had never really succeeded at anything. She had never done anything truly remarkable. Why should this time be different?

That woman would have concluded that God meant for her to give up. Surely the rain and the subsequent storm were no coincidence. She would return to whatever life she could create for herself. Perhaps she'd try to work things out with Jerry, even though she knew with nothing resolved their love itself would finally die. Perhaps she'd get a job. Perhaps she'd continue to run up her credit cards and travel around the world with no sense of purpose or direction—because nothing had changed for her.

She had never believed in something so much that she would risk her life to accomplish it. She wouldn't have stayed here.

That woman did give up. She died in the storm.

I lived. I am who she could have been.

I am my own second chance. Why I deserve it, I don't know, but I'm not about to turn it down.

"I think I should stay." I brace myself for the argument, but Bret and Dana simply nod as if they expected my answer.

"If that's what you want," Dana says, "you better take this." She slips out of her parka. "It's supposed to keep you alive at twenty below. Bret can keep me warm on the way back to the truck."

"I couldn't," I start, but I know she's right. I need it.

"It'll help," Bret agrees. "I've gotta say, though, that I'm concerned you're going to run low on firewood mighty quick."

"You're right," I say. "I've already burned two of the dead junipers and I don't know what I'll do when the other two are gone."

"Your shelter gives me an idea," Bret says. "I've got a wood-burning stove—a tiny one is all—but it puts out good heat for a fraction of what you'd burn in a campfire. Dad used to take it when he went trapping. He likes to brag about how he'd fire up the stove, open the tent door as wide as it would go, strip naked, and laugh at the snow falling all around. Might be just the thing for your shelter. It'd be two or three days before I could get it up here, and I'd have to rig up some kind of stove pipe. I'll look around on my work bench. Maybe I can find you some staples."

I can't help but hug them both; first Bret, who responds with a shy pat on my back, and then Dana, whose tinkling laughter feels warm against my ear.

Fifteen minutes after their arrival they leave me alone once again. I hear the snow crunching under their footsteps long after they disappear into the shadows. Where once the snow lay pristine, it is now marked by the day's melting and by two trails of footprints; one set entering the canyon, the other headed out. How quickly worlds change, even in the desert where change occurs so slowly. In a blink of an eye "one" became "three." In the next wink, "three" returned to "one."

The changes are catching up with me. I'm exhausted. My feet are in agony, alternating between numbness and sheer torture. I remove one Reebok, then the other, and prop them on a rock by the fire. Steam rises almost at once to hiss its own brand of song. My socks are next in my striptease. That's as far as I go, I tell the fire.

I heat a fry pan of water on the propane stove. Not too hot, I remind myself. Tepid. One after the other, I put my feet in to soak. I welcome the pain as they slowly warm. Pain is a good sign. I could feel a needle if I jabbed it in my heel, so things can't be too bad.

I watch as darkness settles over the canyon. The first star twinkles in the velvet blue sky and the moon sheds a gentle glow on the towering canyon walls, turning Pisa Rock as white as bone. I study the jagged cliffs; my campfire couples with the moonlight to transform rock ledges into noses, indentions into eyes. Eyes that watch me. Eyes that know something I don't. Faces in the cliffs, as old as time—perhaps the work of the same witch who ages ago turned the giant into stone. Perhaps I misjudged her. Perhaps she wasn't evil at all. Perhaps she simply couldn't bear the thought of being alone.

Chapter Eight

The only proof I've slept at all is that I remember short, tortured glimpses of a dream from which I've suddenly awakened covered in cold sweat. The details vanish, leaving only vague impressions of being chased into dark tunnels, running in slow motion, unable to get away, but I can't remember from what. I lay in the darkness hearing only my own breathing, terrified of the silence that by day is merely unsettling. I am relearning what I knew all too well as a child: night magnifies all fears.

Between the rainstorm and the blizzard I had no opportunity to fear anything except the weather, but now that those immediate dangers have passed, my mind has fixated on the creatures of the desert that I'm convinced lurk just beyond my shelter. Watching. Listening. They surely know I'm awake from the pattern of my breaths, the quickening of my heartbeat, waiting for me to show myself at my most vulnerable moment. It is the mountain lion I fear the most, though I'm convinced fox and badgers and skunks are equally ready to pounce. My dad would say I'd be *lucky* to catch a glimpse of any of them—a rare chance to observe wildlife in its natural surroundings—but I have no wish for such an opportunity. This is their world and they might not like that I'm in it. Despite the mounting pressure in my bladder, I would not leave the shelter before the protection of daylight if my very life depended on it.

Without the air mattress only the canvas floor separates my sleeping bags from the bare ground, ground as cold and hard as a slab of ice, cold so bitter that it creeps through every fiber of the sleeping bags until it finds my flesh. That the bags are still damp doesn't help. Whatever heat my body manages to produce is usurped by the moisture. Down near the bottom where the inner bag also soaked through, my feet have no prayer against the cold. I have wrapped them in Dana's parka but it isn't enough.

I realize that I have never really known what it is to be cold until now. At Girl Scout camp the hardiest among us started our mornings with a polar bear swim, a plunge into the waters of the Puget Sound before the sun had warmed even the shallows. Cold. Shockingly cold. Our screams from the shore woke the other campers, sensible enough to have opted for an extra half hour's sleep. Five minutes was all anybody could last. Then we'd hop to the beach, wrap towels from head to toe as our bodies convulsed with cold and race for the showers. Fifteen minutes after the plunge we were warm again, ready to brag over a breakfast of pancakes and scrambled eggs just how tough we were. We never considered what would happen if we couldn't jump out of the frigid water after five minutes.

This type of cold, the kind that now seeps through my sleeping bag, is almost worse. It won't kill me, but it won't give me a moment's peace. Not even sleeping in my clothes diminishes its effect. Not even sleeping with my hat on.

Last night's campfire almost turned the tide in my favor. Last night's campfire also consumed the last of the dead junipers. I don't have the energy to look for wood that might have been kept dry under the heavy branches of live trees. I have hardly any energy at all. I suppose it's from lack of sleep, but I've had too little sleep before and not felt nauseous and weak. I probably wouldn't even move except for the pressure that's now becoming pain in my bladder. It's a relief when the canvas begins to glow with the first rays of dawn.

The canvas triangle, the so-called door, hangs limply from the nail tacked to the center beam. Now it strikes me as truly pathetic, both in terms of keeping in warmth and keeping out potential predators. The same so-called door, however, played a leading role in my night terrors. *A mountain lion could walk right in like he owned the place and I'd be in no position to argue.*

If I'd had my druthers, I would have built the shelter to ceiling height so I could stand up straight at least in the center. In fact, that had been my original plan, and I thought the measurements I gave the hardware man who cut the two-by-fours provided the necessary footage. Somewhere in the translation of raw materials into a finished product, however, the shelter ended up being less than five feet tall. I'm five foot eight.

I rise to my knees, push the front flap aside and duck through the opening before the opportunity to stand up straight occurs— and surely that accounts for my sudden dizziness when I do. It's not just a slight spinning. Everything goes dark for a second or two, and my knees quit working. I grope for the shelter to keep from tipping over. A minute later I feel steady again. The heap of my red nylon tent still supported by the lumber remnants goes from fuzzy to clear, and I take a few steps forward to test my legs. Then I continue on past the tent to a particular place behind it— just beyond the northwest corner of my self-imposed territory— and I squat to the ground.

Of all my family's camping excursions, only one required the use of the folding potty chair—the summer we canoed down the Missouri River in Lewis and Clark's footsteps, the summer I lived in fear of being bit on the bum by a rattlesnake and dearly appreciated the boost the potty chair offered. I didn't for a moment consider it cheating. As I assembled my supplies for this retreat, I considered packing such a device. Except for the fact that I could have converted it into a standard chair—and though it wouldn't have been comfortable, I could have at least sat on something other than the ground—I am *so* glad I didn't bring it. I now realize I would have felt like an absolute fool.

I can picture it now. There's me, out in the middle of the desert, sitting on a potty chair with my pants to my ankles. Actually, I have a pretty good idea what I'd look like because I was once in a remarkably similar situation.

My family lived about eight blocks from the elementary school where I attended kindergarten, and I walked to and from school with four neighbor girls. Problem was I had trouble with my bladder. Sometimes I couldn't make it home after school without wetting my pants. I'd show up in tears because the neighbor girls, naturally, made fun of me. *Debi, Debi, can't hold her pee pee.*

"If you have to," my mom said, "hide in the bushes and go."

Sure enough, the next day I felt that terrible urge in my bladder but my mom's advice had neglected to include the possibility that there might not be bushes. As it happened, the route home necessitated crossing an open grass field crowded with giant junior high kids in the middle of football practice. My friends and I were halfway across the field and I was desperate. I'd never make it to the other side. And then an idea popped into my head: It had rained that morning and I'd carried an umbrella.

So I walked just as casually as I could away from the neighbor girls, toward the sideline on about the forty-five yard mark. I opened the umbrella, set it on the ground, ducked behind it, hoisted up my skirt, pulled down my underpants and began the deed. I must have been about halfway through when the neighbor girls grabbed the umbrella and ran.

Their gales of laughter would have been bad enough. The teenage football players, the cheerleaders practicing on the far side of the field, most of my five-year-old classmates and their brothers and sisters in the higher grades—nearly, in fact, every person that comprised my little kindergarten world—they all saw me and laughed, chanting *Debi, Debi, can't hold her pee pee.*

I wonder what all those kids are doing now that they're grown up. What happens to junior high football players and cheerleaders? I wonder if they remember that day, and I wonder if they remember me as clearly as I remember them. Maybe they'd be surprised to see me now. I'm still squatting on the ground. At least, I want them to know, I have the dignity not to sit in the middle of the desert on a potty chair.

The only problem now is that the ground is too frozen to dig a hole. Fortunately, I only have the liquid variety to vent—and I realize that's all I've had to do since I arrived. No surprise, I suppose, as I count the number of meals I've eaten. There was the bowl of rice and chickpea lentils the first night and . . . and . . .

I haven't eaten in three days?

I raise to my feet and again I'm practically overcome by dizziness. I grab hold of a juniper waiting for the darkness to pass, waiting for my legs to work. This time it takes a full five minutes, and even after the nausea rumbles in my stomach.

Yesterday after Bret and Dana left I moved the propane stove into the shelter along with the coffeepot, but I forgot the coffee grounds in the tent. A cup of coffee might help warm me up. After exposing my bum to the wintry blast I can't seem to stop shivering.

I crouch in front of the tent and work the zipper open. The coffee can—I opted for the three-pound size—is just inside the door. I get it, raise to my feet, and this time the world goes totally black.

I don't bother to hold on except to minimize the impact of the fall. Later I can only guess that I stayed there over an hour, but I don't remember how I got back to the shelter. I don't remember how I got back in my sleeping bags. I don't remember how long I lay there.

When I wake up I remember that I haven't eaten in three days. I also realize that in the entire time I've been in the desert I've consumed less than a half gallon of water. I'm dehydrated, nature's oldest trick in her book. People die from dehydration a lot more often than they die from blizzards.

Second chances at life aren't granted every day. For someone who's supposed to be saving herself, I can't believe I'd be so stupid.

❧

DAY 6, NOVEMBER 16, AFTERNOON

Two or three days—that's when Bret said he would bring the woodstove—so maybe today. When I now wake to darkness, the sleeping bag is stiff around my mouth with the frozen accumulation of my breath's condensation. The wind is as ever-present as the cold; both are inescapable. For the past forty-eight hours the cliffs have constantly whined as air rushed through every crevice. Worse, with each gust the canvas loosely tacked to the frame practically explodes like a sail catching the perfect current, filling with air like an instant balloon, so intense I'm amazed the shelter remains on the ground. Following each explosion the canvas doesn't merely settle back against the frame but instead implodes with equal force; the slap of canvas against wood is so loud I can't help but wince. Over and over, explosion, implosion. I long for the silence I once dreaded.

Only the hope for heat—Bret's *promise* of heat—keeps my spirits above the freezing point, but even still I don't know that the heater will provide any more relief than a single tin can could bail out a sinking freighter. I've eaten three bowls of rice and chickpea lentils, and I've forced a constant stream of water down my throat. The nausea has passed, but I remain weak. I've soaked my feet in warm water but they remain stubbornly cold. I've had to relinquish Dana's parka. It's now stuffed in the biggest of the shelter's many gaps in a futile attempt to keep the wind at bay.

I think I hate this place.

I'd like to get my hands on those outdoor fanatics who claim we should all become *one with nature*. At one, indeed. Whoever started the rumor that nature is all bliss and rapture and inner peace neglected to include such trifling realities as scorpions and poisonous snakes and lightning and tornadoes. Show me a woman who's *at one* with a blizzard and I'll show you a dead woman.

These people that tout nature's goodness, are they the same folks who cram their RVs into a thirty-foot concrete space that adjoins eight million other concrete spaces—and call that being *at one?* Eight million and one RVs, each with its portable satellite, cute little awnings dangling Japanese lanterns, a ten-by-twelve piece of Astro Turf spread out on the ground so they don't dirty the trailer's plush carpet with nature—is that *oneness?* Because if it is, I could go for a little of that right now.

How could I have felt so free three years ago when I crossed the desert the first time? Free? I have never felt so imprisoned in my life. I don't want to leave the shelter. I don't dare. At least within these flimsy walls I can pretend that it's not out there—*it,* the desert. Oh yes, it's there, playing with my mind, trying to separate me from what I've always known and have always been, so that the world from which I came seems farther and farther away, almost as distant as the memory of my dreams when I awake.

I am the desert, the wind whispers. *I am as the world was before Your Kind arrived. You invented your own world to replace me, a world of occupations and governments and bureaucracies and social structures and moral systems and religions. You think your world is real, but you know nothing of reality for you know nothing of me. How have you convinced yourself that land can be bought and sold with money—as if money is real, as if it is possible to own a piece of the universe? How have you convinced yourself that morality is real— as if it is possible to be right?*

I toss and turn in my sleeping bags trying to shut out the wind.

You think you are right? it howls. *The sun shines on the farmer's fields and gives his crops life. Is the sun right? Should the sun feel proud? Now the sun beats on the farmer's back and covers him in sunburn. Is the sun now wrong? Should the sun feel guilt?*

I try to resist but I can't. The sun isn't right or wrong, but right and wrong do exist. The desert, encouraged by my ignorance, moves in for the knockout punch.

The coyote eats the farmer's lamb. The farmer shoots the coyote. Which is right? Which is wrong?

I don't know.

Is it wrong to kill?

Yes.

So the coyote is wrong?

The coyote kills to eat.

So it is right to kill.

No, it is right to eat.

Then the farmer is wrong.

He kills to keep the coyote from eating his sheep.

And yet the coyote is right to eat.

Yes, but the farmer has to eat too.

Then both the farmer and the coyote are right to kill even though it's wrong to kill, because the need to eat transcends morality?

If I arrive at the right answer perhaps the wind will quiet. Perhaps the desert will leave me alone.

Yes, the need to eat transcends morality.

How do you know? the wind shrieks and I feel another layer of myself peeled away as if all I have ever known and accepted is crashing down around me. But I will not give in. This is not my world. I am civilized.

And yet I feel savage.

My body smells of dirt and sweat, for even in the cold certain crevices perspire; certain crevices exude their fluids. I smell my-self, knowing that my odor carries on the wind until it reaches soft, wet nostrils sniffing the air for evidence of prey. My hair isn't short enough, matted against my head under my hat. My clothes are crumpled, for there is no difference between day and night attire.

I wonder if my son would be ashamed of me. I wonder if he would even recognize what I've become in only six days in this place.

When James and I were married, I rarely left my house with-out full makeup. I wore expensive clothes. I even attended ward-robe classes for helpful hints on the rules of mixing and matching and making the most of accessories. I learned such axioms as "one must *never* wear pantyhose under open-toed shoes when one's toe nails are painted," which I immediately internalized, along with the other tips, as Truth. When I saw a woman at Sears whose nylon-covered toes flashed like cherries between the open slats of her sandals, I turned to my son and whispered, "how *tacky.*"

That's the mother Tony knew until I left Denver after the publishing seminar and stayed in the one-room cabin in the Sier-ras. The cabin lacked shower facilities so I bought a blue ban-danna and tied it over my head gypsy-style. The third night I drove twenty miles to the nearest town for a pizza fix. The hostess sat me in the very center of the crowded restaurant, surrounded by laughing teenagers and strained parents and wailing babies—all of whom seemed to go instantly silent as I walked into the room. I didn't imagine their curious stares, nor could I deny that I would typically be the first to judge a lone dirty woman with no makeup and a blue bandanna tied around her head—in *public*—as weird. I wanted to stand on a chair and say "this isn't how I usually look." Instead, I sat in silent humiliation, wondering what every person in the room thought of me.

The next morning I decided I *had* to have a shower. I had to look and feel like *me* again.

"The closest shower is at the YMCA," the owner of the cabin had told me at check in. "They'll let you use it for five bucks."

I've never felt so embarrassed as when I walked up to the counter at the YMCA and asked to use the locker room. Only the homeless shower at the Y—if they can spare the five bucks. I didn't *feel* like a confident, intelligent woman. I felt like a homeless waif. I didn't know how much lower I could get. Right about then, I knew I'd never again care if someone painted her toenails bright red and wore nylons under open-toed sandals. I told myself that only the most frivolous of mothers could indoctrinate their children with such garbage, and I determined my son would not grow up with ridiculous Truth planted in his mind.

The summer after I finished cooking at the camp for kids, I took Tony to Canada and on to Alaska. A week of living in a tent later, we needed a shower. I felt no shame checking into the YMCA. My son felt no shame either.

But I am so grateful that he's not here to see me now. I've gone way beyond the boundaries of cleanliness that even the Y could accept. I've gone beyond all the boundaries of human dignity that I've ever accepted for myself or my child. If he were here I couldn't take care of him. I couldn't take care of my own son because I can hardly take care of myself. How is that supposed to make me feel about the goodness of nature?

I'm afraid of what will happen to me if the desert has its way.

I'm afraid to see myself through its eyes. It doesn't care if I'm dirty or clean or how I dress or if I have friends in high places or whether I live in a mansion on a hill. In the outside world such things define who I am. In the desert they are mere pretensions, facades, foreign currency that doesn't spend.

The desert doesn't care who I think I am. It knows only what I really am. It has snatched the umbrella away and once again I am alone in the middle of the field feeling the absolute terror of being exposed.

I wish Jerry were here. He would fix the shelter and he would comb the canyon for firewood. He would lay down beside me and keep me warm, and he would rub my feet until sensation returned. He would tell me not to be afraid of the wind, and he would sit up at night keeping watch while I slept. He would take care of me because I cannot. He would be everything because I am nothing. That's what the desert has proved that I am.

In just six days the desert has proved that I am nothing.

Chapter Nine

The canvas walls lie flat against the wooden frame, at last still. The wind has abated and the perfect silence has again returned. The lengthening afternoon shadows cast by the junipers outside my shelter slowly encroach like mute soldiers who surround and then take the entire canvas. Each day it's the same. They win without firing a single shot.

I no longer attempt to fight back. By day I spend hours on end writing in my journal, warming lentils and rice for lunch and washing the few dishes, but when the sun goes down I allow the desert to swallow me completely in its darkness. I don't light the lantern. I don't light a fire. Both could be seen miles away from the desert floor below the canyon. From the moment Bret and Dana told me about Squirrel Man, I've wondered who else might reside in the desert and who among them might wish me harm. Night transforms the question into obsession.

Perhaps it is because the blizzard pushed me so close to death that I fear it more than ever. Each night I die a dozen deaths as my imagination pushes me over the edge of rationality. A pebble falling from the cliffs becomes an avalanche that buries me alive. A growl in my stomach becomes the angry snort of the mountain lion; a twig rubbing against the canvas of my shelter is the claws of his attempted entry. Worst of all, though, are the sounds I can't yet hear, the sounds of the Midnight Stalker's footsteps stealthily creeping up on my shelter, closer, closer, and when I finally hear them it will be too late.

James used to say I was paranoid. Sometimes after we watched the eleven o'clock news and went to bed and everything got quiet, a dog somewhere in the neighborhood would bark. My ears would come to instant attention and I would hold my breath, listening for another dog to answer.

"James," I'd whisper. "*James.* There's somebody out there." The Midnight Stalker. Each night my imagination contrived a different face; sometimes a jagged scar ran down his left cheek, other times he only had one yellowed front tooth. Sometimes he limped like the Hunchback of Notre Dame, other times he slipped through the streets like a breeze. Sometimes I pictured him wearing a trench coat with deep, bulging pockets. Other times he wore a tailored suit. Only the sharp glint in his eye might betray his true intent. No matter how he appeared in my mind, his aim was always the same: cold-blooded murder.

"I don't hear anything," James would say.

And then the dog would bark again and all the terrible images I had seen on the news that night would chase away any doubts I might have entertained. Sometimes I'd get so scared I'd make James get up and check around the house. Usually that convinced me everything was all right and I'd take myself to task for having been so silly.

But one night the dogs didn't stop barking.

"James," I whispered, shaking his shoulder. I was so sure something was wrong that I didn't wait for his answer. I crept down the hallway to Gina's room and peeked in through the door. A street light outside her window lit the second-story room almost as bright as day, but on this night the walls echoed with swirls of blue light as well.

I tiptoed past Gina and leaned near the window. Three police cars were parked at the end of our driveway, and at that same moment an ambulance pulled up. Its lights swirled too, but none of the vehicles had sounded their sirens.

It didn't occur to me to wake James, nor did I consider going outside. I somehow knew something horrible had happened and all I could do was stand frozen at the window and watch the scene below.

The police, armed with flashlights, began searching the dark street beyond my driveway. Radios cracked and beeped as the beams of light criss-crossed back and forth. The ambulance crew perched on the police cars' hoods. One medic yawned.

And then one of the flashlight beams stopped near a cluster of bushes. Someone shouted and all the beams of light flashed in the same direction and the ambulance crew jumped off the hoods. From my vantage point I couldn't see everything the police saw. I only saw the feet sticking out from under the bushes.

It's strange how the mind deals with shock, for in that instant all I could think of was the scene from *The Wizard of Oz* where Dorothy's house lands on the Wicked Witch of the East. The ruby slippers on red-striped legs are all that's left of her.

This guy was wearing tennis shoes. No one tried to take them off.

By then the neighbors began to filter from their houses like wide-eyed Munchkins. In the presence of Glenda the Good—in this case, armed police—we all took tentative and curious steps toward the bush until the coroner's van pulled up and the officers shooed us back. We huddled around in groups of three or four, some of us introducing ourselves to our neighbors for the first time.

"We'll have to get together sometime," one neighbor said, "like a block party or something."

"I'm moving just as soon as I can sell the house," another neighbor said. "Ain't safe here no more."

"It isn't safe anywhere," a woman in a pink bathrobe said. "Don't know how I'll sleep nights knowing what's happened right here on our own street. What happened, anyway?"

The next morning we heard all about it on the news. Two men had argued over a woman. One man hit the other over the head with a baseball bat. Skull crushed with one blow. I was glad I'd only seen the feet.

The femme fatale had called the police and they'd arrested the murderer, who told them where he'd dumped the body. That's why the police hadn't used their sirens. It was only coincidence that my street was where X marked the spot.

For several days afterward I glued myself to the TV, and when one newscast finished I flipped the dial until I found another. I wasn't looking for further information about our murder, as I came to call it. I was obsessed with all murders. All violence. All evils. All Midnight Stalkers in every form they take.

And then one day I quit watching the news because I couldn't stand it anymore. I quit reading the newspapers too. I didn't want to hear or read about the awful things people did to each other, as if by blocking it out I could pretend it didn't exist.

To a great extent the avoidance technique worked. Since then I've camped alone, hiked alone, driven cross-country alone, stayed in houses alone, and although I don't deny I've sometimes slept with a hatchet next to my pillow, neither have I cowered in fear.

But I'm cowering now.

I tell myself I'm far safer here from murderers than, say, on a street corner in the Bronx—but I would never pitch a tent on a street corner in the Bronx. For all I know the desert is *crawling* with half-starved lunatics who would spot my fire and know there is bounty free for the taking. Or maybe joy riders out in the desert for a cheap thrill, turned ugly and vicious by too much beer . . .

I'm defenseless except for a hatchet. It's too easy to picture my own feet, cowboy boots with curling soles, sticking out from under this shelter. It's too easy to imagine that the Midnight Stalker has got wind of me at last and waits only for the hour of his namesake before he attacks. I wish I could convince myself the danger is only in my mind, but I have seen the proof. And so each night I huddle in my sleeping bags refusing to even strike a match against the night, disgusted with my fear yet unable to believe I'm wrong to be afraid.

DAY 9, NOVEMBER 19, LATE AFTERNOON

Two or three days, that's what Bret said. It's now been six, and as the sun begins to set I realize he's not coming today either. Maybe he couldn't find the stove or he could have had trouble rigging up a pipe. I'm sure he has other things to think about than this, anyway. He could have simply forgotten.

I fight to keep my imagination in check, but I can't help fearing that something has happened to him. Maybe he couldn't keep Dana warm when they hiked back to the truck and she got sick, deathly sick, and he's sitting by her bed in the hospital. Even if they made it back to the truck, they could have slid off the icy road. They could be dead, and I'd never know. No one else knows where I am. What if they never come back?

The first of the shadows begins to creep over my shelter, and I shiver with cold dread for the coming night. For five days I haven't left the shelter except to relieve my body of its wastes, a necessity that I've noticed has become less and less frequent. It's been over a week since I've eaten anything other than rice and lentils, and my body seems to be adjusting to its diet of pure nutrition without the niceties of processed sugars and fats. This is probably how humans were meant to eat, but at night I dream of French fries and onion rings and mozzarella sticks as if my mind seeks to fill the void any way it can.

Nearly all that I have ever considered normal is now gone. From the luxury of constant warmth and tasty food to the relative security of life behind lockable doors; from hot and cold running water to flush toilets; from light at the touch of a switch to televised company at the touch of a button—it is all gone. I sometimes wonder how much of my identity came from my environment. Would I be the same person had I always lived in the desert and never known anything of the world beyond? Is there an "essence" of me capable of transcending my life's experiences, such that I would be "me" regardless of the circumstances of my upbringing?

I reach for my journal, for it is this kind of question that distracts me from dwelling too long on the fear that awaits sundown, like a black-hooded executioner. My journal has taken the place of a mirror in the quest for my soul.

Days ago, I started with my name.

My name was spelled *Debbie* until eighth grade, the year I learned I had a little French in my ancestry in addition to English, German and Welsh. I thought *Debi* looked more French, so I announced the change to my parents and friends. Four years later nobody remembered when I used to be Debbie.

When I married James I accepted his surname. It took me a long time to get used to calling myself something else—as if changing my name changed who I was, and I suppose in a way it did. After about four years I couldn't remember when I used to be single.

And then I divorced.

I could have kept my married name, especially since that would always be my son's name. But I wasn't married anymore. I could have returned to my maiden name, but I wasn't the same person I'd been before I married. Even before I left the one-room cabin in the Sierras I knew I wanted a new surname, one that reflected both my new life and my roots. After long and careful thought I adopted both of my grandmothers' maiden names: *Holmes* from my dad's mother, *Binney* from my mom's mother. The name became legal the same day as the divorce.

It's been three years and the repercussions are still haunting me.

Most of my family respected my decision even if they didn't entirely agree with it. My grandfather, however, thought that by rejecting my maiden name, which happened to have been passed to me through him, I meant to reject *him*.

"I don't understand you," were his last words before he quit speaking to me. He had hit the roof over the divorce, anyway. My name change was just the straw that broke the camel's back.

I said fine, if he didn't want to talk to me he didn't have to, but the truth is it hurt to my very core and still does. We've been close my whole life. I was the first grandchild, and Grandpa always made me feel like his little angel. We spent many an afternoon taking turns reading aloud to each other. I sat on his lap, and whichever of us wasn't reading would follow along on the page.

That Grandpa encouraged reading aloud was no surprise. For more than fifty years the family has gathered on Christmas Eve to hear him read Charles Dickens's *A Christmas Carol*. My grandfather's mother initiated the ritual and Grandpa continued it; now it's been going on nearly seventy-five years. When the army sent Grandpa to the South Pacific in World War II, my grandmother mailed the book, five and six pages at a time, so that Grandpa could read it to his fellow soldiers. He still gets letters from some of them every Christmas, less now as the years have claimed their lives. They say they've never forgotten that he helped them remember the spirit of love and peace on earth on that special day of the year, even in the midst of a war.

I suppose most families have rifts too deep to heal. My grandfather is too stubborn to change his views, and I don't see why I should apologize for doing what I thought was right. Still, I wish I could have talked to him about coming to the desert. He might have understood my need more clearly than anyone else. In his early twenties he was an avid mountain climber credited with several first ascents in the Sierras. Grandma said he was never happier than when he hoisted on his climbing gear, but she couldn't stand it. She told him that she wouldn't sit home and wait for the news that he'd fallen off a cliff. He could climb mountains or he could marry her. One or the other.

Selfishly, I suppose, I'm glad he chose Grandma. If he had fallen off a cliff before my dad was born, I myself wouldn't have had the chance to exist. I can't help but wonder how much of my grandfather flows through my veins, how much he has influenced the person I am.

I'm so deep in thought that at first I hardly notice the sound. It is faint and pleasant and so familiar that it doesn't occur to me to question it until I suddenly remember that the sound does not belong to the desert at all. I set the journal aside and turn my ear toward the shelter door. It's a radio playing pop music. If it were only a little closer I would recognize the song because I can almost make it out now.

My heart gives a startled extra beat before I realize that the radio can only mean one thing. Bret played his at nearly full blast when he brought me to the desert. Finally, he's returned with the stove! I grab Dana's parka from its post in the largest crack and duck outside, zipping the jacket as I practically run the half-mile down canyon to its hidden narrow entrance.

Sound travels well in the outdoors. The number one rule when my family camped was *keep your voice down*—hard to do when you're a kid let loose to play in the woods. It's true, though. Late at night we'd hear the college students' parties. Even clear across the campground we could make out exactly what they were saying and usually what they were doing too. Sometimes we wished we couldn't.

So it doesn't surprise me that I don't see the truck right away.

What does surprise me is that I don't hear the rumble of its engine or the grinding of its tires attempting to maneuver the passage. And the radio has stopped. But then it starts again.

During the next ten minutes as I keep my eyes glued to the canyon entrance the radio starts and stops, never any louder than before, but never any quieter. Far away but not too far. Gone and then it's back, and I am totally mystified. If Bret was coming, he would be here. If the radio isn't coming from Bret's truck, where's it coming from?

I wait another five minutes but the sun is getting so low that I don't dare wait any longer. The half-mile return trek looks a lot further now that I'm headed uphill. Since I got here I haven't been so far from my site and certainly not so near to dark. I pick up the pace as my heart beats a little quicker.

The sound of music comes again and stops me in midstep. The hair raises on the back of my neck and every evil image of the evening news I've ever stored in my brain plays across my mind like a VCR.

Until this moment I haven't paid much attention to the terrain that composes the canyon floor, the way the ground rises and falls like waves on an angry sea capped by a foamy spray of sagebrush. Stones as big as my head lay scattered in seemingly arbitrary piles until I notice that each appears to be the end of the trail for some long-ago rock slide. Even as I pick carefully past them, my mind absorbs the reminder that the falling pebbles I hear at night could, after all, present real danger. And so could whoever is behind this radio, and now I'm nearly running across the canyon.

The shelter is still a hundred yards away when I spot it tucked into a dip on the sage-tipped sea. I cover the final distance in seconds flat and duck inside, pulling the canvas door as tight as I can against the opening.

My breaths are shallow and fast as I poise on my knees, cocking my head, urging my ears to listen for even a single pebble bouncing down the canyon. The radio is silent. The canyon is silent, but my worst fear has become a reality. I am not alone here. My mind goes wild imagining who it is, but it can only be one man, the Midnight Stalker, this time clad in rags and grinning with broken teeth as he pulls a rusty knife from his bootleg. He's searching for me. He will find me. He will kill me.

The hatchet feels like a lead pipe in my hand. I raise it above my head and bring it down fast, a practice shot. The blow could crush a skull if I could get one in before he did, but I picture the struggle and I lose.

Debi, a voice pushes through my imaginations, *maybe the radio doesn't belong to a madman. There are a thousand explanations.*

The image of tennis shoes protruding from a bush refuses to budge from my mind and I raise the hatchet again.

Don't let this place turn you into an animal.

An animal. That's what I am.

No, you are much, much more. Use your mind, don't let it use you.

I struggle to understand what that means and then I close my eyes so tightly that my lips scrunch into my nose.

"Close the canyon," I mentally command. "Let no intruders come through the entrance." The hatchet slowly lowers into my lap as I concentrate. I picture a white fence across the opening of the canyon half a mile below my site. It's a magic fence. Nothing, no one, can cross that barrier.

Even as I shut my eyes tighter I wouldn't want to justify what I'm doing to any reasonable thinking person, but I'm too afraid to stop. I have no other suggestions. This plan worked once, or at least I thought it did, but that was different. I was only sixteen. Maybe I only *thought* my mental commands—some might call it imagery—worked on Miss Dindle.

Miss Dindle should have been a private detective, but instead she had dedicated nearly forty-five years to our high school's attendance office. Any absence from class required a note from a parent, exchanged for an official pass to be given to the teacher. With a mere glance at the note Miss Dindle could discern whether the parent's signature was genuine or a forgery crafted by a truant student. When in doubt she would go to her vast filing cabinet and cross-check the signature.

One morning, having skipped my civics class the day before to enjoy an afternoon in the park, I knew my chances of getting the note on which I'd forged my mother's signature past Miss Dindle were slim. Nonetheless, I had to try. My parent's punishment frightened me even more than Miss Dindle's. As she adjusted the wire-rimmed glasses on her nose she peered up at me.

"Orthodontist *again?*" she sniveled. "Weren't you there just last week?"

"Yes, Miss Dindle," I said, wondering how she managed to memorize the exact medical and dental status of fifteen hundred students. "My braces are about to come off and they're fitting me for a retainer."

As she scrutinized the note her eyes narrowed. "You ought to talk to your mother about scheduling those appointments after school hours."

"I'll do that, Miss Dindle."

"Mmm hmm." She wrote me out a pass and I tried not to let my relief show, but as I turned to walk away I saw her place the note aside.

She knew. There was no doubt in my mind. I *knew* that she knew. She would double check the file and I'd be snagged like a rabbit in a lair. My parents would kill me. Two months restriction, easy.

No, I thought as I headed toward class. *I won't let that happen.*

I squeezed my eyes closed and I concentrated as hard as I could.

Miss Dindle, you will not question that note. You will not cross-check it with the files. Maybe a gust of wind will blow through the window and flip the note into the trash. Maybe you'll get a headache and go home. I don't know how, but somehow you will overlook that note.

I never was called back to the attendance office. There could, of course, have been a hundred reasons Miss Dindle didn't catch me, but at sixteen years old I was as prepared to believe that my mental commands had done the trick as I was prepared to believe anything else.

I called it a mental command. Others might have called it prayer. Tonight I'm not sure there's a difference, nor am I sure either really works, and yet I go on with my command. *Close the canyon,* I repeat over and over in my mind. It doesn't matter how it's done. Maybe a mountain lion will tear the intruder to shreds. Maybe he'll slip and break his neck. Doesn't matter. *The canyon is closed.*

I remain on my knees until the wind kicks up, howling high in the cliffs. A soft pitter-patter on the canvas at first sounds like rain, but when I finally find the courage to look outside, the air is filled with swirling white flakes. Perhaps it is exhaustion, perhaps it is desperation to believe, or perhaps it is the truth, but the snow seems to me a small miracle. No one, criminal or otherwise, would venture out in this weather. For the moment, I am safe.

I tuck myself between the sleeping bags and pull the covers to my chin. The wind is like a lullaby and my shelter is a womb. For the first time since I came to this canyon, I'm not afraid of who or what lurks in the night. The canyon is closed.

DAY 10, NOVEMBER 20, EARLY MORNING

A sound I've heard no less than ten thousand times shakes me from my sleep and I instantly sit straight up.

Somewhere beyond my shelter a phone is ringing.

It's not a modern ring—not an electronic whir or a mono-tone blast, nor is it the high-pitched buzz or digitized tune of a cell phone. It's the kind of phone I grew up with, the kind my son has never even seen, the kind that if you take the back off, you actually see a bell. Back then you ordered your phones from the phone company, one of two styles in a choice of about five colors. The wall-mount phone in our kitchen was beige. The desktop phone in the upstairs hallway was olive green—one of the seventies' more popular shades. Both were rotary-dialed.

Astonished at the noise, I scramble to the door flap and push it back.

Last night's snow merely dusted the canyon but I'm sure this is the coldest morning so far. I'd guess it's no more than ten de-grees Fahrenheit. The sage sparkles in the sunlight as my eyes scan the cliffs to the east and then across the gentle slope of the canyon floor where it meets the cliffs to the west.

My cheeks feel the air's sharp bite and I pull the flap closed while I fumble for my shoes, the only article of clothing I lack to be fully dressed, since I sleep wearing everything else. If only Brct had brought the wood stove . . . but I've reconciled myself to the fact that he may never bring it.

As I lace the Reeboks, the phone rings again. According to my ears' best guess, the ringing originates at approximately the same place the radio music did yesterday. Not so close that it's absolutely distinct, but not so far that it's faint. I can't actually pinpoint the direction.

"All right, that's it." I'm startled but pleased at the strength of my voice and I repeat, "that's *it.*"

By daylight it's easier to find courage, and I am absolutely sick of feeling helpless. I'm sick of huddling in my shelter. I'm sick of being scared senseless by radios and phones and Midnight Stalkers. I'm sick and tired of being afraid. If there's someone else in this canyon then . . .

Then I don't know, but I'm going to find out. The dusting of snow has given me an idea. Whoever was here last night and whoever is behind that phone had to leave at least faint tracks.

I'm tempted to perk a pot of coffee before setting off on my adventure, as I decide to call it, but I'm not sure that isn't just an excuse for delay. No excuses, I tell myself firmly as I zip up Dana's parka. The hatchet completes my wardrobe and it occurs to me that, all wrapped up in a giant bundle with a hatchet slung at my side, I look like the Midnight Stalker myself—except I doubt the Midnight Stalker trembles in his Reeboks as I do. I tell myself it's excitement, not fear. No more fear for me.

Despite the parka and my ever-present knit cap, the air is so cold that I shiver as I push open the front flap, proving that my shelter is at least a little warmer than outside—although the cup of water I poured before I went to bed froze into a solid chunk of ice during the night. I come to my feet careful to look that they don't land atop other prints. I'm exceptionally relieved that they do not.

I cup my hand to my eyes, taking in the mountains to the far west—magenta blue, bluish purple, with a cap of peachy glaze. The clouds are melted marshmallows, trimmed in pale pink against the blue sky, but *blue* isn't enough to describe the perfect clarity, the crystal quality, the diamondlike glimmer of the air.

My focus slowly shifts from the vastness of the sky to the desert floor two thousand feet below my canyon. The white there is not a result of snow—none fell at that elevation—but of the saline in the soil. Where the sun shines straight down, it is golden-white, so bright that I must blink fast and look away. But in the shadows the soil is bluish-white, and here and there patches of green are like a spring meadow, as lush as any field of clover.

And then my eyes come once again to the canyon. Blackish-green juniper trees dotted with silver-blue berries tower from the ground on gnarled brownish-black trunks. Beneath the trees, beds of their own needles look like the fur of a newborn fawn, speckled white and yellow-tan. Each sage is its own brand of muted green; silvery-green, yellowish-green, brownish-green, glittering with frost.

Despite the snow even the ground is a hundred different shades of subtle color. Gray stones, grayish-green stones, grayish-red stones, whitish-yellow pebbles, bluish-white pebbles, reddish-brown rocks streaked with brownish-green intrusions, all poke through the thin layer of ice. The beauty of it almost takes my breath away until I remember what I'm looking for.

Ignoring the hair tingling on my arms, I start with the area that concerns me most: the thirty feet in all directions that I've branded my territory. I hardly breathe as I circle the shelter, first keeping my eyes glued to the ground, then darting up to the cliffs and all around the canyon because I can't entirely dismiss the feeling that I'm being watched. The snow is even patchier than I first realized, and I'm not sure there would be any tracks even if an intruder had dared come so near, but then I look behind me and see the unmistakable prints of my own shoes.

I am overjoyed to find no others. At least whoever-it-is hasn't found out where I live.

The search outward, however, offers just as few clues to the whereabouts of the phone, though it does reward me with evidence of some of my fellow canyon-dwellers. A set of deer tracks leads me in a wide circle around my site, and that trail is sporadically crossed by the elongated ovals I recognize as the mark of a rabbit. There are others as well, but I'm not well versed enough to distinguish between the prints of fox and skunk and badger; perhaps all three. Finally I stoop to examine a trail of tiny three-pronged indentions in the snow, and a shiver of disgust runs up my spine. I recognize those, all right. Mouse. Until now I had been able to ignore the fact that they too share the wilderness. I hope the tracks are as close we come to meeting.

I walk as far as the entrance to the canyon. Not a single human print, and I'm totally mystified until it strikes me that perhaps whoever-it-is isn't *in* the canyon. It's possible that the sounds came from the other side of the cliffs, or perhaps on the other side of the narrow entrance that I imagined "closed" last night. If I climbed the cliffs I could see if either possibility proved correct. That option exceeds the limits of adventure I had bargained for, however. One slip on the pebbled slope, one twisted ankle or broken leg and I'd be as good as dead. There's no way I could survive a night out in the open.

I return to the shelter more than ready for a cup of coffee, and as I finally sip the steaming brew I consider where to go from here.

And that's when the phone rings again. My hand gives an involuntary jump and coffee sloshes across my wrist. Tears spring to my eyes as much from surprise as from the instant pain.

"Damn it . . ." Compared with the silence my voice sounds like a shout and more coffee lands on my hand. I reach for the cup of water that froze in the night and hold it against the burned area but the redness spreads anyway. I wish for the hundredth time that Jerry was here. He would take care of me. I watch as a tiny blister forms at the base of my wrist. If he were here. . . .

An earthen dam never gives way all at once, even though to the onlooker it may seem so. Somewhere deep below the surface the first crack in the foundation occurs without anyone's notice. Perhaps years go by with no problems, until the one year when there's a lot of rain, more rain than anyone can remember. When the dam finally gives way, it collapses with a sudden crack and then *gushhh,* tossing debris every which way as the water, now free, roars that it will never be contained again.

I did not know that this kind of anger existed in me. It is pure, raw, unadulterated fury, nearly blinding in its intensity. I am *sick* of wishing Jerry was here. I am *sick* of needing other people to take care of me. It's not like anyone volunteered to come here with me. I called myself stupid because I forgot to eat for three days. I *wasn't* stupid; I was doing the best I could after nearly getting blown off the face of the earth. What *is* stupid is relying on others when I can rely on myself.

I called myself "nothing" because I could have used a little help. I am *not* nothing. I survived without anyone. No one else did it for me. No one else can really do anything for me. It's all up to me. It always has been and it always will be. That's just the way it is and I might as well learn that now. I have learned. I'll never count on anyone again.

With one motion I swat open the front flap and sling the coffee out of the cup. My Reeboks slip on the tiny pebbles that cover the slope, but I'm too mad to care. I'm determined to scale the canyon if that's what it takes to locate that phone.

I climb for at least half an hour before I stop to rest at the base of Pisa Rock. The column is shockingly tall. Even from my shelter it appeared to have the height of its namesake, but now I see that it actually does and it's just as thick around. I look down at my site to see my tent, an obvious intrusion on the natural desert backdrop. The canvas shelter is harder to make out. Nestled between the junipers it is as discreet as a fawn tucked away by its mother.

I feel the panic rise in my throat and Pisa Rock seems to sway back and forth before my eyes. I'm too high. One slip and I'm dead, but I refuse to be afraid. On the ground I spot a juniper limb and it becomes my staff. I hike upward until I must stop for breath again, and my eyes scan the cliffs that line the upper rim of the canyon still twenty stories above my head.

The explosion that rips through the sky is so sudden and loud that by instinct I drop to the ground and my staff flies from my hand to bounce end over end down the slope. I grope to keep the hatchet tight in my free hand as a second reverberation seers through the air. This time I see it—a military jet, skimming so low across the valley floor that from my place in the cliffs I am actually above it, and now I remember.

I saw it on the map before I drove to the wildlife refuge. A huge area outlined in yellow with the words *Public Access Denied* stretching from one boundary to another, the Dugway Proving Ground is one of three adjacent military testing sites that together form one of America's most massive and secret security installations. Its southern border is a mere fifty miles from my canyon.

Another jet now skims the desert floor and the air roars again. I shade my eyes to watch it disappear into the horizon. The thunder fades like a receding storm as the jet returns to the world from which it came, a world so far away that I can't see it or touch it or taste it anymore, and I'm left with a sensation of bitter-sweet nostalgia. In that world mankind has reached for and even attained the very stars themselves, a feat which seems impossible given that for the past ten days I have experienced virtually the starting point of human progress. Mankind elevated itself from the desert's square one. And yet, despite the marvels of its genius, the jet also reveals a side of humanity that is as cold and black as the dark side of the moon. The jet is a weapon of war. People kill in the world beyond the desert, and not just to eat.

When all the water has rushed free of the broken dam, nothing remains but the initial trickle that, once upon a time, was captured and became a reservoir. All around are the signs of the devastation, the earthen dam washed away to become bits of mud and sticks downstream, but the trickle trickles on, bubbling and burbling as if that is all water ever does.

People kill in the world beyond the desert, but at their best people also love. I think my third grade teacher had it right all along. Mrs. Darling said food and shelter and clothing are the most basic elements of life but you couldn't leave out love because that was the hardest one to live without. I'm not the same person who entered the desert ten days ago. That woman didn't know she could rely on herself for her own survival, nor did she realize that that awareness is the very difference between being nothing and something. Even still, I think Mrs. Darling must have been right. Maybe it's good not to need others to take care of me, but without love, life would be as empty as the dry lake behind the broken dam.

Chapter Ten

By the time I make my way fifty feet down the slope to recover my staff, I'm feeling less inclined to retrace the lost altitude, much less go on to climb the full distance to the top. I haven't heard the phone since I started the hike, and the voice of reason, or perhaps exasperation, has begun to kick in instead. There are no telephone lines within twenty-five miles. Still, I know what I heard.

The alternative to completing the climb, however, is no more appealing. The thought of returning to my shelter, always semidark and cloaked in cold and gloom, just to wrap myself in sleeping bags that smell of ten days worth of body odor, just to write in my journal on and on and on almost makes me ill.

Without making a conscious choice, I half step, half slide down the slope until I reach the base of Pisa Rock. On the cliffside where the tower meets the slope there's a semiflat area about three feet wide of solid, exposed stone. An ideal spot to sit and watch the view a while, a view remarkable if for no other characteristic than its stillness. Even the clouds hold their positions as if they've been painted on the sky. The whole vista from one horizon to the other looks like a movie backdrop. It's hard to believe anything so perfectly crafted could be real. I half expect the jets to return, but after at least forty-five minutes I've seen no further sign of them.

Each day the sun rises from behind the high walls of the canyon that I now face, meaning that though the sky grows light at dawn it isn't until much later that the sun finally crests over the cliffs. I've figured out that by that time about a quarter of the day's light is spent. That mark has come and gone. The sun is directly overhead and most of the snow has melted away, save for the few patches still protected by the shadows of the larger juniper trees. Another six or seven hours remain until sundown, and I wish I could think of something to do that doesn't involve chasing noises. My failure to solve the mystery thus far, however, weighs heavy on my mind. I know I have no choice but to climb to the top of the cliffs once and for all.

I take a last, long look at the picture-perfect expanse of desert, magnificent in its silent stillness marred only by a dust cloud. Or maybe it's a dirt devil. I'm not even sure what the difference is except a dirt devil looks like a miniature tornado and this looks more like a miniature . . . cloud. And it's moving. If I'd seen it earlier I might have noticed where it came from. As of now all I know is that it's not far from the entrance to my canyon and every second brings it closer.

It doesn't take a genius to figure out that *something* is causing the dust to spew, and my mind flies to the radio and the phone. Maybe *this* is the explanation. My heart picks up the pace until it feels as loud as the Tin Man beating on his hollow chest. I'm tempted to scramble further up the cliffs but my feet seem to be frozen in place.

But the dust cloud isn't. It disappears for a moment between the folded ridges and I know it will reemerge within my canyon, within *my* canyon, and I remember the magic white fence. I close my eyes and I frantically command *close the canyon,* but I already know it won't work.

I don't know how I know, but I do. Maybe it's because the same command only works once. My first forged note slipped past Miss Dindle, but not the second one even though I concentrated just as hard. That time I'd skipped geometry. I knew even as I mentally said, *"No, Miss Dindle, you will not check my note,"* that she'd gone right to her giant file and compared the signatures. I wasn't surprised when I got the summons to the office later that afternoon. By the time the principal got through with me, I was stuck with five weeks of after-school detention. By the time my parents got through with me, those five weeks of detention looked like a Club Med vacation, but I had known what was coming the minute I left Miss Dindle's office.

So I'm not surprised to open my eyes and see that the dust cloud has cleared the canyon entrance and is now heading in the general direction of my site, but I am startled that I can at last determine what's making the dust rise. Now I can hear the grinding of gears and the rumbling of an engine and a radio blaring full blast, all belonging to a dirty white Toyota. The horn honks a series of wild hellos.

I let out a shriek that ricochets off the cliffs like a boomerang as I practically surf down the slope, pebbles slipping beneath my feet like burned rubber. By the time the truck stops I've reached it and the driver's window rolls down.

"Special delivery," Bret Layman says with a grin. "One wood stove, COD."

"If you'll accept desert dollars." I laugh way too loud, but I decide that's because I haven't had anything to laugh at in a long time. At last, there it is, in the back of the truck. The stove. No bigger than a bread box—perhaps fifteen inches wide and ten inches deep—and it looks *old*. Cast iron, it's no longer black but rusty red. The door, once solid, now boasts a hole about an inch wide. It barely clings to the body of the stove on ancient hinges.

"You been all right?" Bret asks, eyeing me head to toe. I'm glad I don't have the cowboy boots on. One look at the curled soles and he'd probably toss me in the back of the truck and cart me out of here.

"Looks like you've been through a war zone," Dana says, emerging from the passenger side.

"It's been cold," I admit.

A *humph* noise comes from inside the truck and brings a laugh to Dana's lips as she turns back to the Toyota. "What'd you say?"

The sun is in just the right position to reflect off the truck's windshield, making it impossible to see inside for the glare. "You heard me proper. I *said* it's colder than a witch's ass."

"Oh, come out and be social," Dana says with a wink my way. "We didn't bring you along just for your crabby wisecracks."

"All right, then." The voice is accompanied by grunts and groans and a sliding movement across the seat, and then the driver's door opens and a man comes to his feet. He's dressed in overalls, and he's about sixty years old—hard to tell because his hair is snowy white, and though he isn't bearded, neither is his face shaved. He gives a brief nod in my direction and reaches into the truck bed to pull out a six-foot-long pipe, maybe six inches in diameter.

"Where do you want this?" the man asks Bret.

"Over there," Bret points. We both stare after him, carefully dragging the pipe toward my shelter.

"Who . . ." I whisper.

"That's the Squirrel Man," Dana says. "He's spending a few days with us."

My mind races to remember the details. Vietnam. Shot one of our own. Wife left him as soon as her plane landed, and now he lives in the desert and eats squirrels because hunting deer would be poaching. Despite Bret and Dana's ease with him, I can't help but think this isn't exactly the kind of person I'm pleased to have in my canyon. My arms instinctively wrap around my chest, and I don't like the pit that's forming in my stomach.

Why did they have to bring him here? I watch him inch nearer to my shelter, wrestling with my own emotions. Maybe he's harmless enough but . . . but . . . it isn't just a matter of safety. I feel invaded, like this is my spot—my territory, almost like a home, sort of—I guess it's the closest thing I have to a home. I didn't invite this person but here he is ducking his head into my shelter like . . .

"'Scuse me," I call out. "That's kind of private."

If I'd sneaked up and kicked him he couldn't look more shocked. It's the same expression a dog gets in his eyes when he's sound asleep and you accidentally trip over him. Even as he bolts out of the way, he looks at you like he's totally bewildered over what he did wrong.

"I thought this would be where you're wanting the stove," he mumbles and backs away. "Can't see nowhere else for it." Dana and Bret stare in my direction, and I feel instantly ashamed. He's just trying to help, and I practically bit his head off.

"Just let me put a few things away before you go in," I say. "I'd hate for you to see what a slob I really am."

"Don't make no difference to me," the Squirrel Man says, and as I duck past him into the shelter I'm convinced he means it. He doesn't seem the least bit curious of me, as if there's nothing unusual about trucking twenty-five miles into the middle of the desert just to install a wood stove in some woman's canvas shelter.

It takes only a moment to fold up my bedding and push it out of the way. Looking at the bare canvas walls and the bare canvas floor, it sinks in that there's nothing else "private" about my shelter at all. A pile of sleeping bags and a cookstove, a few pots and a coffee cup, and that could belong to anybody. There's nothing that gives even a clue that I, as opposed to anyone else, live here. No photographs, no mementos, even though I brought them with me. They're still in a bag under the nylon tent. I never bothered to unpack them, and just now I wonder why.

"We'll have you set in no time, assuming I figured right," Bret says when I reemerge. He rolls a fifty-five-gallon barrel off the truck. "These here are furniture ends." He reaches into the barrel and pulls out a handful of blocks just the size for the tiny stove. "They'll burn hot but fast." He drops them back into the barrel and grabs his tool box. "I use 'em for kindling at home. They'll get you started but you'll still have to feed it with something more substantial. Here," he tosses two plate-size aluminum disks to the Squirrel Man, "hold these a minute."

Bret, Dana and the Squirrel Man make a skilled team. First the Squirrel Man hauls five or six slabs of rock from the truck, which Bret slides into the shelter. One slab becomes the stove's foundation. Bret places the others to shield the canvas walls from the heat.

Now Bret takes the aluminum disks, each with a six-inch hole cut out of the center. Dana holds one against the canvas on the outside while Bret scrambles inside to hold the other directly underneath. I've never watched anyone "grommet" before, as Dana calls this maneuver, but within minutes the aluminum shield is firmly in place, the canvas is cut within the six-inch circle, wire supports are run from the ground to the pipe and the stove pipe pokes out like a straw from a chocolate milkshake.

"Got any newspaper?" Bret asks, sticking his head out the front flap. A moment later, the first puff of smoke crests above my shelter.

"I can't believe it," I say, putting my hand on Dana's arm. "I just can't believe it."

"Before I forget . . ." she digs in her pocket, "Guess you'll be wanting these." She hands me a staple gun, an extra box of staples, a match-box full of assorted nails and the remainder of the coiled thick wire used to support the stove pipe. I stare at the pieces of molded metal. They're not worth $2.75 in the world beyond the desert. Here they're more precious than gold.

The Squirrel Man hasn't directed a single word at me since the work began, nor have I spoken to him, though I've watched his every step. I've noticed him glance my way from time to time as he circled the canvas shelter, apparently judging my handiwork—or, more likely, the lack of it. I'm surprised when he looks me straight in the eye.

"I reckon you can staple the canvas to the frame," he says. "That'd take care of the flapping." Under other circumstances I might be embarrassed that he honed right in on the shelter's defects, but despite my commitment not to rely on others, the fact remains that my lack of carpentry skills is self-evident. I'm surely not too proud to listen.

"Yep," he continues, "I'd put a staple here." He points to the middle of the crossbeam. "And here, and here, and probably here. Well, maybe not there, but here, definitely here."

"I'll do that," I nod.

"Nice piece of canvas," he says, running his hand along the shelter as if petting a cat. "What'd you give for it?"

"A hundred dollars," I answer. "Army Surplus. There's three tarps altogether."

The Squirrel Man puts his nose nearly to the cloth. "Nice piece of canvas, sure 'nuf." He continues to circle the shelter, peering this way and that. Finally he concludes his inspection and once again looks me in the eye. "Anyone bothered you since you been here?"

I hesitate, not quite sure how to answer. "Not really, I guess."

"Either you been bothered or you ain't."

"A couple of times I've heard sounds," I say. "A few days ago I heard a radio, and this morning I woke up to a phone ringing. I was climbing the canyon to see if I could figure out where it was coming from when you arrived. Do you know of anybody living out here?"

"Ain't nobody else here," the Squirrel Man says. "You ain't been hearing no phone, neither."

"I heard something."

"Now that's a fact," the Squirrel Man nods.

"I don't get it."

"You ever heard of phantom limbs? A man loses his arm or his leg." He makes a chopping motion over his arm and then his leg. "Let's say it's amputated, clean cut off. Damnedest thing. He'll wake up screaming in the night over a pain that's in the arm or the leg—but there can't be no pain because there ain't no arm or leg. You can't tell him that it don't hurt, though, because his mind has compensated for the lost limb and still thinks it's there."

I nod.

"Same way with your ears. Call it phantom noise, if you want to. Your ears aren't used to hearing 'nothing.' Everywhere you've been your whole life, there's something that makes noise, even if it's just in the background. Your ears are almost always stimulated. But here your ears don't have much of a job. When the wind isn't a-blowing and everything's perfectly still, your ears don't know what to make of the situation. So the mind compensates and makes up sounds that the ears are used to."

"Are you sure about this?"

The Squirrel Man snorts. "If you're here long enough your mind will get adjusted. It'll quit making up sounds and then you can hear what's *really* here. Wait'll you hear the music in the fire. You'll think you've lost your mind."

Music in the fire? I search his eyes for some sign that he's joking.

"Maybe you won't hear it," he says. "You're lucky if you do because that means your ears have learned to work again from being so overloaded in the first place."

I want to ask him what he's talking about but Bret's voice interrupts.

"That's about got it," he says, emerging through the front flap. "Don't think the stove'll give you much trouble, just be careful with that door. I soldered best I could, but take it easy when you add wood. And don't feed it too much at a time or it'll smoke bad. Let 'er warm up."

"I was just learning about fire music," I say, hoping the Squirrel Man will shed a little more light, but Bret laughs aloud.

"Can't pay him too much attention," Bret says. "He's liable to twist your arm right off."

"Nobody said you have to believe," the Squirrel Man shrugs. "Ain't my fault you can't hear it."

"I'll grant you that," Bret says.

"You weren't so high and mighty about the BLM, though. Did you tell her?" Bret gives him a sharp look, but the Squirrel Man returns it with another shrug.

"What's going on?" I ask.

Bret clears his throat and watches his foot trace a little circle in the dirt. "After I dropped you off out here I got to thinking . . ."

"*You,* my eye," the Squirrel Man interrupts. "It was my idea."

"All right, it was your idea to check into it," Bret says.

"You got to," the Squirrel Man nods firmly. "Any time the government can catch you in the least little mistake they will, I can promise you that."

"So anyway, I already knew that this canyon is on BLM land," Bret says.

"The Bureau of Land Management." The Squirrel Man's voice rings as if reading a royal proclamation. "Your government in action."

I know all this. Bret assured me there was no problem staying in this canyon. The long-term permit didn't apply here.

"But you didn't *check,* did you?" the Squirrel Man says. "Not until I said you'd better."

Something tells me this isn't going to be good news.

"Turns out this business about long-term permits applies to all BLM land," Bret says. "I still say they wouldn't have granted permission in the first place, but since you don't have it they could legally make you clear out after two weeks. Now don't worry, there's only one BLM representative for this whole district, and I bet I've seen him once. Nobody's going to make a point of telling him you're out here, and there's no other way he could find out. Wouldn't lose any sleep over it, I just thought you should know."

"I hate those bastards," the Squirrel Man spits. "Ain't a one of 'em who don't think they own the whole wilderness."

"Oh, there's some that's all right," Bret says, but Squirrel Man's on a roll.

"Guardians. That's what they're supposed to be. Guardians, my eye. They'd like it best if nobody ever set a foot on their precious land. You can bet, little lady, if they find out you're here they'll take great pleasure in kicking you off—and probably hand you a $500 fine to boot."

"Fine?" I say. "For what?"

"*Trespassing,*" the Squirrel Man spits again. "Trespassing on Public Lands—yessir—Public Lands. Your land, my land, the land that they're *guarding* for us. Hoarding is more like it. Know why they won't let nobody stay longer than two weeks?"

I shake my head.

"They don't want nobody settling permanent like. Now that's about the damn stupidest thing I ever heard. Who's gonna squat in the desert *permanent?*"

"You are," Dana grins.

"I *ain't* on no BLM land." The Squirrel Man looks pained. "Lasso owns his land outright and he gave me legal permission— *legal,* mind you—to occupy that satellite parcel that wasn't doin' him no good anyway."

"Lasso?" I ask.

"Lasso's his nickname," Dana says. "When he was nineteen or twenty he could rope a steer quicker than I can crack an egg. Wanted to be a rodeo man."

"He'd a made a good one," the Squirrel Man says. "It's just tragic, that's all."

"It is at that," Bret agrees. "He was practicing for the regional tryouts when his horse bucked him. Before anybody could get the steer out of the corral, it came right at Lasso. Trampled him. Broke his arm in five places. That was the end of rodeo dreams."

"He's a good man," the Squirrel Man says, "though I've never met a man who has more trouble with cars. I swear that man is cursed. He's never bought a car that hasn't broken down two weeks later. Myself, I'm handy with engines, and I try to help him out because if it weren't for him I don't know *where* I'd live. Sure as hell couldn't squat long on BLM land, and I wouldn't do nothing illegal like. But I'll tell you *what*. Any soul that could survive out here, not bothering nobody else—hell, I got to admire that person."

He looks straight at me, and I feel my cheeks flush at the implied compliment.

"I don't think you'll have any trouble with the BLM," Bret says as he loads the last of the tools in the truck.

"I hope not," I say, but it's not easy to dismiss my feeling of unease.

"Well," the Squirrel Man spits, "if they give you any trouble just tell 'em *I* think they're full of hog wash. That oughta settle the matter then and there."

Despite the potential problem that Bret's information presents, I can't help but smile. The Squirrel Man obviously has no doubts about relying on himself. "It was nice to meet you," I say, extending my hand. The Squirrel Man takes it and gives it a solemn shake.

"Don't forget about the music in the fire." His eyes drift away and come to rest on the shelter behind me. "Nice piece of canvas, sure 'nuf."

I watch the Toyota lumber out of the canyon, the cloud of dust in its wake growing smaller and smaller until at last with a final toot of the horn it disappears behind the folded ridges. I can't prevent the sharp revolt that rushes through every cell in my body at the moment when I become once again entirely alone, and I wonder if the Squirrel Man feels the same reaction after his brief visits with Bret and Dana. It's as if even the body knows that the spirit wasn't designed for absolute solitude.

As I walk back to my shelter, a phone rings somewhere in the distance. I shake my head and stride on. The phantom strikes again.

Chapter Eleven

Mankind took a giant leap forward with the invention of the staple gun.

"On guard," I say, squeezing the trigger. A staple shoots into the air at an invisible foe. "Take *that,* you evil cad." I squeeze again and giggle until I remember that I shouldn't be wasting staples. But I can't help feeling playful each time I glimpse the smoke curling from the new stove pipe. The past ten days have taught me to savor lighthearted moments as long as they last. The desert doesn't give them up easily.

I'm determined to put the Squirrel Man's advice to good use, however, and the canyon rings with the repeated *ka-chunk, ka-chunk* of the staple gun as I tack the canvas snug against the frame in at least a hundred places.

Ka-chunk, ka-chunk, and now the walls don't flap anymore.

Ka-chunk, ka-chunk, and now the triangle flap that has hung loose across the entrance for ten days is trimmed and neat and secure.

After less than an hour's work the result is even more impressive than I hoped. Once merely canvas slung over a frame, the shelter now embodies the confidence of a little cottage. Tucked among the junipers with smoke wisping from the stovepipe, its status has been elevated from a scene out of *The Three Little Pigs* to more like one from *Little House on the Prairie.*

Ka-chunk, ka-chunk, I squeeze the staple gun again and the director's chair frame that has sat untouched for ten days is introduced to its seat, and now I have somewhere to sit. Ten days ago I might not have been impressed by something as simple as that, but ten days ago I had never sat on frozen tundra for ten straight days.

Every few minutes I duck inside the shelter to add a few furniture ends to the fire. Bret was right, they burn hot but fast, and I suspect that without my constant tending it would soon go completely out. I don't mind. The stove is such a novelty that I get a charge every time I open its hinged door and see the flames. The shelter is finally warm.

Surely, surely the worst is now over. If I had known eleven days ago what I was getting myself into, I wouldn't have stepped a foot into the desert. I *have* earned the Squirrel Man's compliment. I *have* toughed it out under conditions that in retrospect seem subhuman, and I don't mean only the cold. As I look around me, I'm reminded just how primitive my living conditions are. Perhaps from the outside the shelter looks cozy and snug, but duck inside and, except for warmth, the illusion is ruined. Not even a bed, not even an air mattress. Just a pile of smelly sleeping bags on the bare canvas floor.

I guess I've been too occupied with survival to worry much about dignity, but now the thought of wrapping myself in those sleeping bags one more night is too much to take. I haul them outside and shake them hard and spread them across some sagebrush to air out.

Fixing the director's chair has given me an idea. In the drum with the furniture ends I find a couple of pieces of boards, one that's three feet long and eight inches wide, and one that's ten inches square.

Tap tap tap, I nail a couple of furniture ends to the shorter board and I've got a little bedside table. It only stands six inches off the ground and it wobbles under pressure, but it's better than what I've had for the past ten days, which is nothing.

The other board fits perfectly along the back wall inside the shelter. *Tap tap tap,* I nail it to the frame and it makes a shelf. I arrange my toiletries—the ones I've had no opportunity to use— and tack a nail in the corner closest to the wood stove for my hand towels, finally thawed from mopping the tent after the rainstorm. There's something so *civilized* about arranging one's possessions on a place other than the ground.

I rummage through the tent for the finishing touch: a photo of Tony in his Little League uniform the day his team won the championship. I was there for the game, one of the few times I've been able to watch him play. He hit a triple and the next batter bunted him in. The pride on his face as he slid across home base brings a lump to my throat even now.

"I miss you," I say, kissing my fingertips and touching them to my son's lips. "Don't worry, everything's going to be all right."

As I back out of the tent a flash of bright red catches my eye. I'd almost forgotten the split gourd Cherokee mask that Jerry made with wide circled eyes—*to watch over you*, he said—and I can't help but sigh.

"I think you'd be proud of me," I say to the mask because that's what I would say to Jerry if I could. "I've come a few steps."

I've got a long way to go.

All afternoon I arrange and rearrange, sorting through the belongings still in the tent and organizing my provisions. I'm taking control in a way I haven't before. No longer will I be victim to the cold. No longer will I live in squalor.

Throughout the day storm clouds have been building in the west and now they cover the sky. The first snowflakes fall just as I finish collecting the sleeping bags. I press my nose against the fabric and breathe deep. The stench is gone and a trace of sage lingers. When I fluff the bags up and spread them on the floor they even manage to look inviting. There's nothing I can do about a mattress, but by now I'm accustomed to the ground anyway.

The desert has proved one thing without a doubt: an entire world can change in the blink of an eye. Yesterday morning I woke to the world of the Ice Age. Tonight, although snow is falling outside, inside I am warm. Yesterday morning my shelter was a frigid tomb. Tonight it is . . . well, for the second time today I find myself thinking of it as the closest thing to a home I have. Maybe "home" is a slight exaggeration, but I find that it lacks for almost nothing. Except companionship. The loneliness seems even more pronounced after Bret, Dana and the Squirrel Man's visit.

I open the wood stove door to add more furniture ends and— just in case—I lean my ear close. I still wonder what the Squirrel Man meant about music in the fire. I don't hear a thing.

But that's not quite true, I realize as I stay still and make an effort to listen. The fire pops and snaps as the flames engulf the fresh wood, sometimes letting out a little hiss. Now there's a kind of sizzle and then a short, low moan. From time to time the stove itself creaks as if stretching its limbs after a long nap; I doubt it's been used for years. All the sounds do create a sort of symphonic complement to the flames, but it would be a stretch to call that music. Perhaps the Squirrel Man meant to be symbolic. At least I haven't heard any more phantom noises, though I suppose it's because my ears have had something to listen to. Between the stapling and the hammering it's a wonder I can hear at all.

But every staple and every nail was worth it.

I've slept under a fair number of roofs in my life, but this is the first place I can say I built with my own two hands. It never occurred to me to *want* to, despite Thoreau's admonition that "there is some of the same fitness in a man's building his own house that there is in a bird's building its own nest." I thought, what's the big deal? Besides, most modern homes are too complex for average people to construct by themselves. Now that I think about it, that seems kind of sad.

As the snow falls and darkness takes over the canyon, I realize that I've improved the situations of nearly everything in and around the shelter except for one thing: me.

I add a half-dozen furniture ends to the wood stove. Bret said they'd burn hot; I'll see how hot is hot. Within minutes I remove my hat and run my fingers through the tangled mess. My scalp is sore and my hair feels and smells like congealed bacon grease. Next off comes my scarf.

A gallon jug of ice melts in the soup pot on top of the wood stove. The water begins to steam and the shelter becomes a sauna.

It's so hot that I can't bear it in my clothes, and for the first time in eleven days I begin to undress. First my sweater, now my flannel shirt. Next the ski pants, then my leggings.

I test the water in the soup pot. Perfect. I place the fry pan on the floor and bend over it. Cup by cup I pour liquid heaven over my head. My shampoo, frozen since the second night, has finally thawed near the stove. Squeezing a bit into my palm, the entire room fills with its fragrance. I've smelled no such scent for so long that I'm nearly overcome by the perfume. No House of Pleasure could smell more sweet, feminine or sensuous than this desert shelter of mine. It is as exotic as a Turkish bath, and I am draped in pale silk, reclining on a satin divan while three stewards massage each inch of my body with oil. Careful, boys, you missed a spot—start from the beginning and do it again.

But it is I who must do it again, for one lather and rinse only gets the first layer of grime. More cups of water, more shampoo, more water, until my hair comes clean to my satisfaction. I rub it with a dish towel and within minutes it dries in the heat. Cropped short and fluffy against my cheek, it is the most delicate fabric in the world. As I dip a towel into the water and wash my skin from tip to toes I am transformed into the most sensuous creature ever to grace the earth. I am a gazelle, prancing through fantasies of ecstasy so intense mere mortals can barely glimpse their pleasure.

I forgot that I could feel so good. Almost reluctantly I finally tuck myself between the sleeping bags and blow out the candle on my new bedside table. As always, I check to make sure the hatchet is within easy reach.

If the past ten days have taught me anything it's that I'm capable of far more than I ever knew. I can take care of myself. I can be tough as nails.

But tonight I've remembered that life isn't only about being tough. I am more than the iron will of survival. I am also as soft as a kiss.

Chapter Twelve

DAY 13, THANKSGIVING DAY, MORNING

This Thanksgiving day does not start out like the Thanksgivings of my childhood or any Thanksgiving I've known since. I wake to no cheerful voices nor the smell of turkey wafting from the kitchen. I wake to silence and to cold. The stove isn't large enough to keep a fire banked over night, so I wake to find the fabric of my sleeping bags frozen around my mouth. Not even a single coal remains of the fire.

But unlike the days before the stove's arrival, this morning I wake to the luxury that within minutes my little home will soon be comfortable. It *is* a home, of sorts, and it's a delight to find that everything I need is within reach. Without leaving my sleeping bag I simply lean over to the wood stove and light the paper underneath a handful of tinder. I lean a little to the left and light the propane stove to heat my coffee. By the time it's brewed the wood stove is hot, filling the entire shelter with the pleasant ambiance of warmth.

Perhaps the desert doesn't care how I look or smell, but I've remembered the first lesson of human dignity. I feel a lot better about myself when I'm clean. I can't spare the water to wash my whole body every day, and I figure I can only wash my hair every ten days, but now I make the effort to at least splash my face first thing in the morning.

I also feel better about myself now that the shelter is clean. Not that it's possible to completely keep out the dirt, but it is possible to sweep it out with a dishtowel at least once a day. It's possible to "make" my bed and wipe off the table and keep a pot of juniper needles simmering on the wood stove to fill the air with its piney aroma. Even if I were to remain alone the rest of my life, even if I were to never see another human being again, I would keep myself and my shelter as clean as I could. The simple act of controlling that one factor empowers me to face other elements of desert life.

One such detail is on my mind this morning. For two days I've burned nothing but the furniture ends Bret brought in the barrel, a barrel that is now a third empty. A wise woman might save for a rainy or worse day. If a blizzard like the first were to hit again and I couldn't get out to forage for wood, an emergency stash could mean my ability to ride out the storm.

My early fires having consumed the dead junipers close to my site, I must now hike further up the canyon. I'm surprised to discover that the canyon is experiencing a slight warming trend. The sun is shining in a brilliant blue sky, not a cloud to be seen, and my breath no longer turns to frost. Only a dusting of snow remains, not nearly enough to carry a sleigh over the river and through the woods to grandmother's house for a Thanksgiving feast.

The best source for dry wood once again proves to be beneath living junipers, protected by thick, heavy branches. The only problem is that though the junipers tend to grow in clumps of two or three, the clusters are several hundred yards apart. The ground between is rocky and uneven and scattered with sage. It's slow going because I have to carry the wood I find under one clump all the way with me to the next, all the while keeping a tight grip on the hatchet. Thoughts of mountain lions are never far from my mind, and although a hatchet might not be much of a defense, it is far preferable to none at all.

Under most trees I find a stick or two, but once in a while I hit the jackpot—an actual branch as long and big around as my leg. The branches are easier to drag back to my site than the smaller sticks are to carry, but I can break the smaller limbs across my knee into stove-sized pieces, whereas the branches must be chopped.

I have grave doubts about the gadget I employ for the job. Axing has never been among my more developed skills, and as far as I'm concerned it should usually be left to professionals. This opinion formed in my teenage years when I witnessed an ax head fly off its handle and arc through air as if the onlooker's forehead for which it was destined had drawn it like a magnet. Thirty-two stitches repaired the forehead but it's fair to say I've been wary of axes ever since.

My skepticism is heightened by my relative lack of physical strength. I chose this particular ax from among the hardware store's offerings because of a sticker on its handle: Boy's First Ax. The store didn't have Girl's First Ax or a Weak Woman's Ax, but I suspected some jobs would be too much for the hatchet so I settled for the safest bet. I seem to have made a suitable choice, for I am actually able to heave the thing over my head. Every third swing or so I even hit the wood, though the other attempts result in an ax head buried in dirt—not the thing, I've been told, for maintaining a sharp blade, but if I ever need a plow . . . .

Once I've axed the branches a couple of times, the "stomp" method finishes the job. I rest one end of a log on another to lift it several inches off the ground, and then slam my foot down on it. When the logs splinters, the results are stove-sized pieces. When the log doesn't splinter, the impact jolts my entire leg.

I'm sweating hard now, and I brush a fly from my face. It takes me a second to realize that this is the first insect I've seen since I got here. It must be forty degrees outside, a regular heat wave. Even the ground is thawing a bit, leaving my site a muddy mess, and I regret swatting the fly. That's no way to treat my only companion.

"C'mere, little guy," I coo. "I won't hurt you." But the fly zips away. I decide to name him Felipe because I have this thing about naming animals. In fact, I sort of have a thing about animals in general.

Growing up, my house was known as the Zoo House, thanks largely to my father's job, after he quit teaching college and before the move overseas, as curator of education at the Point Defiance Zoo in Tacoma, Washington. Between zoo babies rejected by their mothers and Dad's reputation as "the person to call when you find an injured animal and don't know what to do with it," our house gave refuge to a number of furry friends over the years.

One Friday, Dad came home with three baby lions, and my sisters and I cuddled them all weekend. I still wonder if Dad checked with Mom beforehand, because our kitchen was already serving double-duty as the temporary home for a baby pygmy goat. The goat strained us all, particularly Mom. Not only did we trip over the chicken-wire cage that took up half the kitchen, but the goat required eight bottle feedings a day, four of them in the middle of the night—Mom's job.

The goat wasn't my mom's only problem, nor was the kitchen the only room inhabited by a "guest." The bathroom also gave shelter to another critter. Actually, the critter *reigned* over the bathroom. He was a river otter, rescued after Mount St. Helens erupted volumes of ash and mud into nearby streams. The woman who found him knew it was illegal to keep wild animals, but it was obvious that the otter would die without immediate help. The ash and mud in its fur had turned as hard as cement. Dad was given special permission by the state to bring the otter to our house, but it was Mom who got in the bathtub with the nearly lifeless creature and picked every trace of hardened muck from its fur. It was Mom who watched him around the clock those first few days, and it was Mom who fed him.

That might explain why she was the only one the otter allowed within fifteen feet of him after that. I personally resented the otter's territorialism, given that our bathroom was significantly smaller than fifteen feet. I'd put it off as long as possible and then make a mad dash for the toilet. The otter—we named him Ornery—splashed out of the bathtub and sped across the floor to bite whatever happened to be vulnerable. So as soon as I sat down, I held my feet high off the ground and, essentially, prayed.

Animals were such a natural part of my environment that I hardly thought twice to find a dead woodpecker in the freezer or a glass cage of shrews or a garage full of rabbits. My friends always said that I had a really cool house and really cool parents, but to me it was just normal. Even though I've never outgrown my fear of snakes and mice, that's also probably why I can't help but name the fly. It's all my parents' fault.

I miss them so much. Today of all days.

It wasn't just a coincidence that I tried to make that first Thanksgiving dinner I cooked for James extra special. Having been married just fifteen months, I was trying to lay the foundations for what would become our family's traditions. James came from a tradition of watching football until two o'clock when dinner was served, followed by watching football until six when turkey sandwiches were served, followed by watching the highlights and replays of all that day's games until everybody—well, I anyway— was bored by seven.

The Thanksgivings of my childhood were entirely different, though at the time I looked forward to them with about the same enthusiasm a cat regards a bath. I believed that the addition of either Halloween candy or Christmas presents would have gone a long ways toward improving Thanksgiving, for the esteem in which most people hold The Dinner completely escaped me. The only part of the turkey I considered edible was the skin. I despised stuffing, and as for pumpkin pie, I considered it a tragic waste of an otherwise perfectly good crust. My Thanksgiving dinner consisted of as many sourdough rolls as my plate would hold, as much crispy skin as I could get off the bird in one piece, and olives. I'd put one on the tip of each finger and then suck them off, slurping as loud as possible before Dad gave me "the look."

Mom and Dad considered Thanksgiving a prime opportunity to invite company, usually at least a dozen people who might have otherwise spent the day alone. The second year we lived in

Washington, Dad invited the Laos, a Chinese family who had just moved from Shanghai. Mr. Lao was a university professor. Dad said, "Their daughter is about the twins' age, and their boy is just a year older than Debi! Mrs. Lao is bringing a *Chinese* dish— won't that be *fun?*"

The one thing I despised more than stuffing was Chinese food. I dreaded the Laos's arrival. When the doorbell rang, Dad herded us together, opened the door and shouted "Hello!" so enthusiastically that had the Laos not been too stunned to move, they would have turned and ran. Finally, Mr. Lao, blushing bright, pressed his hands together and bowed. "Ah hallo."

Mr. Lao spoke about first-grade English. His wife, son and daughter spoke not one word. What I remember most about that dinner, besides my father's valiant efforts to break the near total silence, was what each child chose from the buffet table. The visiting children heaped their plates full of rice and their mother's vegetable concoction. Not a trace of turkey, nor stuffing, not even a spoonful of gravy. My sister's plates, however, boasted all the traditional favorites and none of the Chinese veggies—and on mine, ten olives and six rolls. My father, of course, raved over Mrs. Lao's vegetables, and Mr. Lao bobbed his head when he tasted Mother's turkey. But we kids knew the truth: some things just don't mix.

Following dinner, our tradition every year was to play games— cards, board games and one that may have originated in my household: Plunger. In this game all players except one place an empty thread spool tied with a string into a common heap just big enough to fit under a toilet plunger. One player is assigned the plunger, and he or she holds the plunger about two feet above the pile of spools. This player also rolls the dice. The first roll establishes "the number." Thereafter, whenever that number comes up on the dice, the players with the spools must jerk theirs from the pile before the plunger smacks down and traps them in. If any player pulls his spool on a number other than "the number," he or she is out. The last player out becomes the plunger person for the next round.

Given the language barrier between us and our guests, cards and board games were clearly inappropriate. However, my father managed to mime the object and rules of Plunger to Mr. Lao, who then interpreted to his family.

My dad has probably the best laugh in the whole world, and he uses it frequently to fill an entire room. His sheer delight and total lack of restraint sets his laugh apart from any other that I've ever heard. And when he laughs, he attempts to yell out whatever he finds so funny, as if it's necessary to shout to be heard above the laughter—which it actually is.

I am amazed by Dad's ability to fake his laugh. With my grandfather's health progressively failing, it is now my father who reads *A Christmas Carol.* There's a scene during the Ghost of Christmas Present, in which Scrooge's nephew Fred bursts into laughter. If Mr. Dickens could only hear the bellow my father attributes to Fred, he would rest assured in his grave knowing he had inspired the very soul of Mankind. It starts out low in Dad's chest, comes to his throat, turns into a near fit of coughing-laughing-gasping for air, ending as a wheeze. If tears aren't by then actually running down my father's cheeks, which often they are, the audience is sure they were running down Fred's. It takes Dad as long to recover and continue on with the story as it would have Fred to find his composure.

I believe it was Dad's laughter that most perplexed our Chinese visitors. When Dad, at the helm of the plunger, rolled "the number" and slammed the plunger down, trapping all of the spools before even one of them made their escape, he burst into a laugh that would have put even Scrooge's nephew to shame. The Chinese children stared at him open-mouthed, as if such public displays of levity were totally foreign—which they likely were. Mr. Lao managed to get into the swing of things: he smiled broadly and bobbed his head when it came his turn at the plunger. Mrs. Lao only observed, her hand covering her mouth to hide her amusement—or, possibly, her horror, I wasn't sure.

The next Thanksgiving, I was surprised when the Laos again accepted Dad's invitation. We hadn't seen them even once during the interim, and didn't the next year either, though they again showed up. In fact, they appeared for the next ten Thanksgivings, until my parents and sisters moved overseas. Each year, Dad opened the door to shout "Hello!" in his exuberant way. Mr. Lao always bowed with his hands pressed together, "Ah hallo." Mrs. Lao always brought a Chinese dish.

And over the years her dish became the hit of the party. My taste buds matured to love stuffing and gravy and even pumpkin pie—and Chinese food. The Lao kids matured into Chinese-Americans and heaped their plates with as much turkey as tofu. Their English, of course, became flawless, and when we played Plunger, even Mrs. Lao joined in the laughter.

The entire time I was growing up I never realized that some—if not most—people spend their Thanksgivings in front of the television watching other people play games. I thought everybody invited company that would have otherwise spent the day alone. I never knew just how meaningful my parents' Thanksgivings had become to me until I tried to create a memorable Thanksgiving for someone else—someone who had his own traditions and his own memories and didn't want to replace them with mine.

Just now I don't blame him. I guess I wasn't willing to replace my traditions with his, either. I didn't realize that to an amazing extent we *are* our memories. Perhaps the highest goal of partnership is to not disturb what we've been before, to not deny what each has been until we met, but to forge new traditions that rise from the still warm ashes of both our pasts.

Strange that I'd have to spend a Thanksgiving all alone in this desert canyon before I could come to such a simple understanding. Still, it's hard to imagine Mom and Dad and my sisters playing Plunger without me.

I can't help but wonder what the Laos would think of my desert Thanksgiving feast. For thirteen days my diet has consisted solely of rice, lentils and a vitamin pill. My mouth is already watering at the promise of pumpkin. Felipe has returned, buzzing around as if he knows a treat's in the making.

It seems only fitting, given all the rolls that graced my plate on Thanksgivings past, to at least substitute them with a morsel of bread. I brought flour with me, though without leavening, sugar, milk or eggs, I'm as liable to end up with glue as bread. I decide that kneading the dough serves no advantage. I simply mix it with my fingers until the batter sticks together when I pat it between my hands. After I have six of the flat, palm-size loaves, I place three at a time in the frying pan, coated a quarter-inch deep in oil.

Within moments, a delicious odor rises from the pan, and Felipe zips in through the open door of my shelter for a peek. "Bonjour, mon ami," I greet him with my best French accent. "Walcum to zee Desert Cafe. Table for one?" The fly lands on the corner of the propane stove as if waiting for the opportune moment to dive. "Watch it," I warn, swishing him away. "Hot oil." Felipe buzzes around the stove and shoots out of the shelter.

The bottoms of the fry-bread loaves are golden brown, and I flip them over. The oil sizzles as I marvel at how such basic ingredients as flour and water can combine to create this incredible aroma. I swear, no kitchen in the country smells any better on this Thanksgiving than my canvas shelter. If I tell myself that often enough, perhaps that will help chase away my longing for Mrs. Lao's Chinese food.

When the loaves are browned on the second side, I take them from the pan to cool while I open the can of olives. I duck out of the shelter into the sunshine, hoping to spot Felipe. I settle into the director's chair, my lunch on my lap. I dip a chunk of bread in the olive juice and pop it in my mouth.

"Mmmm," I moan, "you're missing out, Felipe. Come on, don't pout. Eat up, for tomorrow the bread may be gone." I crumble a bit of the loaf on the table. All right, so the crust is as tough as hardtack. At least it's not lentils.

In moments I hear a familiar buzzing and Felipe zooms into view. "'Bout time," I say, as the fly settles on the bread crumbs. "Wait'll you see *this.*" I reach into the bowl of olives, and put one on the tip of each finger. "The louder you slurp, the better."

As the fly instantly buzzes to land on an olive, it occurs to me that Felipe has never tasted either bread or olives before. If I hadn't come to this exact spot in the desert, his brief life would have gone untouched by human intervention. For all I know, by giving him a taste of the outside world I've altered his entire life. This one tiny morsel of olive might even motivate him to leave the desert in a desperate search for just one more taste before he dies.

I retrieve the can of pumpkin along with a spoon and settle back in the chair. I scoop out a bit for Felipe. "Live a little," I encourage the fly.

Chapter Thirteen

Felipe retired hours ago to wherever flies retire, and I am once again alone. I try to occupy myself with happy Thanksgiving memories, but instead of cheering me up they only punctuate my isolation. Loneliness is a particularly mean aggressor, luring its victims along brightly lit lanes with fond reminiscences and tender times. No one can venture down that road without eventually being forced into the shadows.

Tonight the wind rustling high in the cliffs seems to sing eerie lamentations, mourning for some lost soul, and I can't help but fear it's mine. Somewhere, somehow, I must have strayed far off course to have ended up here in the desert alone, and now I wander through my memories to find the error in my judgment. There are, of course, many mistakes, some more consequential than others. I ran away from home when I was seventeen. My parents grappled with what to do with me for most of my teenage years. Despite the promise of the wonderful future I envisioned for myself, I gave my folks a pretty good scare. I was difficult, rebellious, moody and uncommunicative, nothing like the sweet angel who once ran to her father's lap and begged to be read a story.

I was so determined to be independent from them. I wanted to make up my own mind, and so, starting when I was about fourteen, I did. If I knew they wouldn't allow me to go somewhere or do something, I told them I was going somewhere else.

It's a dangerous thing when your kid starts to lie. After you catch her in a couple of whoppers, you can't trust that she's ever telling the truth. I don't remember how they caught me, except once. I was supposed to be going to a play with Mark, a guy from my church youth group. Neither of us were old enough to drive, so we took a bus downtown. We arrived before the theater opened, and because our church was just across the street we decided to wait there on the steps.

Perhaps the setting itself encouraged our discussion. We began to talk about God. We agreed that hell was an outrageously outdated myth, concocted a couple of thousand years ago by the same kind of people who believed the world was flat and the sea was inhabited by green monsters. It made no sense to devote our lives to avoiding an eternal fate we didn't believe existed. We had to be meant for *more.*

Two young minds, two young hearts, exploring life's mysteries, and the world around us ceased to exist. Before we knew it, the theater doors opened across the street. The crowd, however, wasn't entering the theater: they were leaving. We had missed the play.

When I got home, my parents asked me how I'd enjoyed the drama. A queer feeling came into my stomach when they asked me what it was about, and I sort of mumbled an answer. Turns out that at the last minute my parents had been offered tickets to the same play. They'd been shocked not to find me there, worried half out of their minds.

In exchange for one of the most special nights of my youth, I got a month's restriction. An intelligent teen might have seen the value in telling the truth in the first place, but it took me about another five years to figure it out. In the meantime my parents rarely believed I was wherever I'd promised to be, and usually they were right.

It seems to me that some people struggle with growing up. Some people can't play by their parents' rules. Some of those people never make it as adults, and I think that's what scared my parents the most. Fortunately I outgrew my youth and my parents forgave me for it, at least most of it. I don't lie to them anymore. I try never to lie at all, even to myself. But I'm still asking the same question I asked that night long ago on the church steps. What am I meant for? Since I've been here in the desert I have sometimes thought I was getting closer to the answer, but tonight I have to face the truth: I'm not sure I really am.

There is no moon at all and it is as dark as a tomb in my shelter, though nothing specific causes the shiver that runs down my spine. I hear no noise I can't explain. The occasional pop is the fire in the wood stove; I stoked it extra full before I got into bed. The whistle in the cliffs is the wind, just the wind, and yet it is as if some restless phantom rides on that breeze, unable to find peace of mind. The air has more the feeling of Halloween than Thanksgiving.

It's been fifteen years since I had to memorize Edgar Allen Poe's *The Raven* for an English class, and I'm sure that if at any time since someone had held a gun to my head and said "recite it or die," I'd be dead. Thus it seems particularly curious that as I tuck myself between my sleeping bags the poem begins to run through my mind.

> *Once upon a midnight dreary, while I pondered, weak and weary,*
> *Over many a quaint and curious volume of forgotten lore,*
> *While I nodded, nearly napping, suddenly there came a tapping,*
> *As of some one gently rapping, rapping at my chamber door.*
> *"'Tis some visitor," I muttered, "tapping at my chamber door—*
> *Only this and nothing more."*

The poem rewards me with a genuine case of the creeps. I swear I actually hear the gentle tapping at my shelter door.

> *Presently my soul grew stronger; hesitating then no longer,*
> *"Sir," said I, "or Madam, truly your forgiveness I implore;*
> *But the fact is, I was napping, and so gently you came rapping,*
> *And so faintly you came tapping, tapping at my chamber door,*
> *That I scarce was sure I heard you"—here I opened wide the*
>   *door;—*
> *Darkness there, and nothing more.*

I'm sure I hear something. Perhaps it's started to rain. That would explain the pitter-pattering on the canvas, and the need for an explanation is suddenly pressing. I scoot from my sleeping bag and peer outside. I hold my palm flat out. No droplets fall on it. Phantom noise, I tell myself. Even so, I could have sworn I heard it, like tiny footprints.

> *Back into the chamber turning, all my soul within me burning,*
> *Soon again I heard a tapping somewhat louder than before.*

> *"Surely," said I, "surely that is something at my window lattice:*
> *Let me see, then, what the threat is, and this mystery explore—*
> *Let my heart be still a moment and this mystery explore;—*
> *'Tis the wind, and nothing more."*

It isn't the wind.

I sit up in my sleeping bags and strike a match. Is it my imagination, or does a shadow dart across the shelter wall? I fumble for my flashlight and shine it all around. The propane stove with two pans atop it appears as I left it after washing the dishes. Did I leave that plastic fork on the floor? Yes, clumsy of me but I must have. Everything else looks normal, just as it should.

I add a few more sticks to the wood stove and close the cast-iron door before flipping off the light. I lay awake an hour or more, however, with Poe's rhyme running through my mind: *'Tis the wind, and nothing more.*

I don't know how long I've slept when I'm jolted awake. I'm confused. I can't figure out why I woke up. Maybe I have to go to the bathroom, except I don't. Then, I hear it—the same type of faint tapping as before. Go back to sleep, I tell myself, it's only phantom noise. Just like the phone.

But then I hear it again and the hairs on the back of my neck stand straight. Go back to sleep, I urge myself, dreading the idea of lying awake hours in the night, hours when I'm sure to hear a dozen other sounds I can't explain, but it's too late, and seconds later the noise comes again. This time, it's more of a scurrying sound, as if something's moving softly across the floor.

Phantom noise, I try tell myself, but I don't believe it, and now I'm really scared. This is when I would tell James to go check out the house. This is when I would be terrified that the Midnight

Stalker would already be hiding in the closet ready to get me before James got back.

I flip from my back onto my stomach and bury my head beneath the covers leaving an opening just wide enough to breathe. And then, I *feel* it. On my head—*tap tap tap*—like tiny reindeer. There's no such thing as tiny reindeer, I remind myself, as the horror sinks in. There's something on my—

Bolting straight up, the something is flung into the air. I grab the flashlight and flick it on in the nick of time to catch a glimpse of a thin gray tail disappear behind the propane stove. My wail is no less than a banshee. *Oh, grroooooooss gross gross gross it was on my head.*

My shelter has been invaded by a mouse.

Day 14, November 24, pre-dawn

The several hours I sit stiff-backed, waiting for the sun to rise, afford ample leisure to examine why it is, exactly, I can't convince myself to lay back down and go to sleep.

Although it is true that I've been afraid of mice ever since my dad kept the cage of the ones he studied for his Ph.D. in my tiny half-bedroom when I was three years old, the fear has never approached phobic levels. I don't think, in fact, that I'm really *that* much more afraid of mice than most people.

Snakes are something else altogether. I'm terrified of them. I don't even like to look at them in pictures, and if I'm watching a movie and somebody falls into a snake pit with hundreds of serpents all slithering around, I shut my eyes until the victim is either rescued or snaked to death. If I ever dropped into such a pit I would have a heart attack on the spot.

But I'm not *that* afraid of mice. What I don't like is their "startle factor," like back in the grocery store when the mouse suddenly darted in front of my shopping cart. Everything about mice is sudden. I don't like that they suddenly *appear* and scurry around *fast*. If they'd just slow down a little it wouldn't be so bad, but they don't. And they're always unexpected. It's impossible, really, to anticipate what a mouse will do.

That's why, while I wait for the sun to rise, I don't lean over to start the coffee. The last I saw the mouse he was disappearing under the propane stove. If I disturb the stove I might disturb the mouse, and he might suddenly *appear* and shoot right past me or run around in circles. That would bother me immensely.

That's why I don't light the wood stove, either. It went out long ago and I'm practically freezing, but it's possible that the mouse crept out from under the propane stove when I wasn't watching, and maybe he's now behind the wood stove, and if I disturb him . . . .

Maybe I'm wrong, but I really do think it would bother most people to be in a contained area with a disturbed mouse. Especially when it's dark. Not that people have always been able to avoid it. During the Middle Ages everyone but the most wealthy slept on hay scattered over the floor. Mice lived in the hay too. Must have been a trick trying to sleep with them flitting around all night, but apparently people managed back then because I guess they really had no choice. Maybe they didn't think it was that disgusting.

But I do. I can hardly think of anything more revolting than mice crawling all over me, especially when I'm asleep. What if it got into my sleeping bag with me? And I also suspect that people in the Middle Ages were largely ignorant of the role rodents played in the spread of disease, but I'm not. A mouse wouldn't go out of his way to bite me, but then again, if I'm having to fling him out of my sleeping bag there's no guarantee that he wouldn't be startled enough to defend himself.

Not to mention that he might be startled enough to poop. Bites and poop, that's how diseases spread. It is *definitely* not a good idea to sleep with a mouse, definitely not, and that's why I can't go back to sleep.

When dawn finally breaks I begin the task of emptying the shelter. I still haven't seen a sign of the mouse—Little Sport, I name him—but I have to be absolutely sure that he's gone. While I'm at it, I scrutinize the shelter for possible entry points. The most likely spot is at the back wall, where the two pieces of canvas overlap. It's so loose that any mouse worth his cheese would consider it an open invitation. In addition, the corners aren't tight, and the front flap isn't secured at the bottom. With a sinking stomach, I now see plenty of places where the mouse might have slipped through.

As the sun steadily slips across the sky, I spend all afternoon stapling. The canvas is now so secure on the frame that the Squirrel Man couldn't get it off in one piece even if he had a mind to carry it away, which I suspect he does. Nonetheless, I suspect that a truly determined mouse could find a way in. At least it won't be through the front flap. Using the last scrap of the two-by-fours, I staple the bottom of the canvas to a board that can swing open and closed as needed. When closed, it's essentially crack-free.

Although I'm more grateful than ever for the staple gun, I've revised my initial assessment of its place in evolution. Human progress made a giant step forward with the invention of the staple gun, but the ascent most surely began with the mousetrap.

In the world beyond the desert, today marks the day after Thanksgiving, and people are flocking to the malls. I can almost smell the caramel corn mingling with perfumed soaps and candles and cinnamon, each shop contributing its own flavor to the aromatic feast. I can almost hear the canned Christmas carols, piped through the high-ceiling central corridor, played over and over again as merry shoppers hum and step along in time. The mall is a wondrous and enchanting mouseless world of laughing children, toy soldiers and drums, sparkling lights, where even the most whimsical dreams come true on Santa's lap. I wonder if he could make *my* wish come true.

Please, Santa, kill the mouse. Because *I* can't do it. I can't even catch him, and even if I could, how would I kill it? Beat it to death? Me, the animal lover? Me, the vegetarian? It's not like I'd be thrilled to kill a mouse even if I wasn't.

My grandfather practically blew his lid when he found out I quit eating meat. That was one of the few times he broke his code of silence after I changed my name.

"I suppose you think it's more healthy," he said, peering at me over his glasses.

"Not really," I said. "Fish is good for you."

"Then I guess you're some kind of animal rights activist." He pronounced "activist" with the contempt he normally reserves for the word "environmentalist"—which has always struck me as ironic because I doubt there's anyone any more environmentally conscious than my grandfather, who served as a forest ranger once he gave up mountain climbing. I think maybe the war protesters in the sixties—those damn hippies, he used to call them—turned him off to all forms of activism.

"I'm not an activist," I replied. "I don't care what other people eat."

"Then *why?*" Grandpa boomed.

Now, I've met vegetarians who I'm almost certain believe they are one step higher on the moral ladder than eaters of flesh. They consider themselves to be just a tad superior, in other words, and maybe that's their rightful reward for not getting to enjoy the pleasure of chicken fried steak. But I don't feel that way at all. If anything I'm embarrassed about why I quit eating meat. I told Grandpa that I couldn't justify that other people had to kill animals on my behalf since I couldn't kill a cow or a chicken or a pig myself unless I was starving. Grandpa just groaned, an Archie-Bunker-meets-Meathead kind of a groan.

But I didn't tell Grandpa the whole story. He never would have understood. I really became a vegetarian because of a snake.

Because I grew up in a city and because that city was in western Washington, one of the few regions of the United States that is not home to venomous snakes, the only danger of encountering a viper occurred whenever I visited my dad at the zoo. Except for one instance when I tried to overcome my fear of snakes by allowing a boa to slither up my arm, a tactic that in no way improved my estimation of it, I steered well clear of the reptiles.

It wasn't until I went to Alabama, rural Alabama, that the chances of coming face-to-face with a *serious* snake improved. Black snakes, as the locals call king snakes, commonly grow to six feet, and I've heard stories of chicken snakes twelve feet long and as big around as the stovepipe that now sticks from my canvas shelter. There are tree snakes and whip snakes and blue racers, and worst of all are the rattlesnakes and copperheads—especially the copperheads because they give no warning before they strike.

Given that everyone I met in Fort Payne, Alabama, boasted at least one snake story in their repertoire, I realized it probably wouldn't be long before I too would have one of my own. I became obsessed with putting off the event as long as possible. That Jerry had built his cottage in the woods sharply increased the odds that I would encounter a snake there. The six-inch layer of leaves and detritus on the ground provided nearly perfect camouflage for almost every kind of snake. Thus, it was quite likely that not only would I encounter a snake in those woods, I might actually stumble upon it. To stumble upon something is to experience the startle factor at its absolute most startling, increasing the risk of both bites and heart attacks exponentially. I therefore decided to rake trails, three feet wide, into and through the forest. Then, if there was a snake along the way, at least I could see it.

If anyone ever wants to find a snake, probably the best way to go about it is to rake around in the undergrowth. I tied bells to my ankles and stomped my feet and yelled *shoo* to warn any that might be sleeping out of the way. As Jerry sat at his word processor, I inched my way deeper and deeper into the woods. Hardly a moment went by when I wasn't thinking about snakes.

One afternoon Jerry and I took a drive through the countryside. I was at the wheel. As often happens when driving through the countryside, my mind sort of drifted and I wasn't paying particularly close attention to the road. I barely registered the stick laying in the middle of the pavement up ahead, so I didn't understand what Jerry meant when he pointed and said, "Hey, look out." I had rolled right over the stick before I realized it was a black snake. I looked in my rear view mirror to see its pale yellow underbelly raised to the sky, a sure sign that it would not survive to the other side of the highway.

"You meant to hit it, didn't you," Jerry said. "Just because you don't like them."

"No," I said, "it was an accident, I swear." I felt horrible. If the snake had been a puppy I wouldn't have regretted the loss any more. I had *killed*.

As a kid I once poured salt on a six-inch banana slug and watched it die a truly slow and gruesome death as the salt sucked every bit of moisture from its membranes. That's the only thing besides bugs I ever killed intentionally. I'd been so obsessed with avoiding snakes that when I managed to kill one, which is the direct opposite of avoidance, I believed the event was more than coincidental.

I'm not sure that animals have spirits, but I'm not sure they don't. If they do, I figured I had offended that snake in the worst way possible. It occurred to me that if I felt so bad about a snake's spirit, maybe I should consider the spirits of the animals that died not by accident but because I wanted to eat them. That's when I decided not to eat them anymore, but I'm still kind of embarrassed about it.

But the mouse presents a problem. He's obviously not stupid; after all, it only took him three nights to find the warmest spot in the entire canyon. He probably caught wind of my fry-bread, or maybe Felipe spread the word. I suspect that Little Sport will be back, and I suspect that I will have great difficulty convincing myself to go to sleep.

I wish I had a trap. The only idea I can come up with is the "fork under the frying pan" trick. If I tie a string to a fork, prop up the pan with the fork, and put bait underneath, when the mouse comes I can pull the string—the pan will fall—and the mouse will be trapped underneath. Unfortunately, I only have that plastic fork, and only dental floss for string. I soon discover that the fork wasn't designed to prop up a frying pan. Time after time it slips, but I keep trying until it's balanced. Finally, I find a few crumbs of fry-bread and the trap is ready. Not that I exactly know what I'll do with him if—I mean *when*—I catch him. Can't let him go, obviously. Guess I'll keep him in my coffee can until I get ready to leave. Just what I need. A pet mouse.

As darkness falls, I prepare for the imminent capture. As always, I tuck the hatchet near my pillow and place the flashlight on my tiny bedside table with a candle. The trap is set between the propane and wood stoves, and the three-foot floss, attached to the fork, stretches thin across the shelter floor. I tie a little loop at my end and secure it on my left thumb.

I wriggle into my sleeping bag, taking care not to inadvertently tug the string. I blow out the candle, roll onto my stomach, pull the covers over my head, and leave a hole just big enough for my nose and eyes to peek out.

Before I've even said my prayers I'm jerked to attention by an unmistakable scratch. There is no doubt that the mouse is already *in.* I'm so shocked that I raise straight up, the floss goes with me, and the trap bangs to the floor as the fork flies across the room. I shine the flashlight in each corner. No mouse there. I shine behind the stove. No mouse.

And then I spy him, crouched in the corner. His shiny black eyes sparkle over a little baby nose. In the second before I grab the hatchet, I swear his eyes reach out to me, begging my understanding—begging *please let me stay*—but in the next second I'm filled with horror and disgust and I *bang* the hatchet on the ground and yell, "Shoo, get out of here!"

He scampers into the shadows along the shelter wall.

"Shoo!" I shout, pounding the hatchet against the shelter's frame. He's probably getting a kick out of this. It's his new game: Scare the Hell out of the Camper. I wonder, if I put a little bowl of food just outside the door, maybe that would satisfy him. Sure, and tomorrow night he'll bring his zillion brothers and sisters for the handout.

I hear the pitter-patter of the mouse again. I bang the hatchet and yell, but now the scampering continues and I realize it's not the mouse. The soft *pit-pat* grows louder and louder on the canvas above my head and I rejoice to realize it's rain. Perhaps the storm will rage so fierce that Little Sport will seek the safety of his own den. I reset the trap and then, finally, I can sleep.

Hours later, I'm jerked from a light slumber by a crash of metal. I snap on the flashlight. The frying pan lies flat on the canvas floor. I tap on the pan. No scurrying underneath—and that makes me wonder. I tap again. Still no response. I summon my courage and raise the pan no more than an eighth of an inch. I hold my breath, waiting for a tiny claw or a tiny nose to poke out. Nothing. I dare to raise the pan a little further, and then completely off the ground.

The crumbs appear to be undisturbed. I must have pulled the string in my sleep, but now I'm not sure I'd hear the mouse even if he did go for the bait. I decide to place a sheet of aluminum foil under the frying pan and put the crumbs on the foil. If the mouse gets near the bait I'll hear his little paws make a metallic tap, sure to wake me up so I can pull the string.

Four times in the night, the trap jolts me awake. Four times in the night, I answer false alarms. By morning, I am disgusted and exhausted. Beyond that, sometime in the night the rain turned to snow. Poking my head out the shelter's front flap, I'm amazed to find the ground covered with five inches. The three pronged tracks that circle my shelter do nothing to bolster my spirits.

Chapter Fourteen

I wait until the first rays of light seep into the shelter before I scoot, still in my sleeping bag, across the floor to light the burner beneath the coffeepot. Opening the wood stove door, I spread last night's ashes across the bottom, crumble a newspaper and lay on a few sticks not much larger than matches.

This is one cantankerous stove, and it is particularly stubborn today. It is an especially cold morning, so cold that as I bend to blow what I hope will be life into the small mound of paper and twigs, my breath is a cloud of white fog. The paper lights, not with the burst of flame necessary to engulf the twigs, but instead only around the edges, slowly burning toward the center, smoldering for a few moments before it goes out. I must now start over, scoop away the twigs, wad another piece of newspaper, replace the twigs, strike another match.

As smoke curls beneath my successful second attempt, the

coffee begins to gurgle. I reach to lower the gas before the pot boils over, which I've learned by experience happens about two seconds after the gurgle starts. If I miss the opportunity, coffee shoots from the spout to splatter all over the stove, drowning the burner, which then sputters and hisses the next four times I light it.

I've coaxed the fire to a self-sustaining level—at least for five minutes, when it will require its second feeding—and with my coffee brewed, I scoot back across the floor to recline against the back beam of the shelter. My hand seems unsteady as I raise the mug to my lips. Maybe it's shaking from the cold. The coffee, however, is too hot to even sip, so I lean forward to rest it on the tiny bedside table. It's then that silver flashes across the floor.

Curious, I crawl from my sleeping bag, careful not to disturb the coffee cup. I moisten the tip of my index finger and place it on the silver sliver, bringing it close to my face. For a moment I can't place the shiny material. And then I know, except it still doesn't make sense. And then I have an idea why it might make sense, but I don't want it to. My eyes dart to the frying pan, still poised for action on the tips of the plastic fork, the floss still winding over the floor to the head of my sleeping bag. It can't be, I would have heard it. I was sure I would, and so I allowed myself to believe it was safe to sleep.

The aluminum foil I placed under the pan, the foil I was sure would alert me to the pitter-patter of the mouse, is in shreds like a mound of grated silver cheese. My hand trembles as I reach for my coffee cup. I stare at the propped-up frying pan, sipping my coffee, trying to calm myself, and then I remember the desert handbook on the shelf. Sometimes a little education goes a long way.

I'm glad the handbook has color pictures because fifteen

different types of mice reside in the Great Salt Lake desert. Little Sport is not a Dark Kangaroo Mouse or a Pale Kangaroo Mouse or a Chisel-Toothed Kangaroo Mouse or a Western Harvest Mouse. What I noticed about my mouse was his face, and now that I see the picture I agree with the name. Little Sport is a Deer Mouse, and beneath the picture is a description. My stomach goes hollow as I read: *Beware all interaction with this breed of mouse as they may be carriers of the Hanta virus, incurable and often fatal to humans.*

Now my entire body shakes. The mouse was on my *head.* He could have pooped on my hat. I swept the shelter floor with a dish towel. Did my hands contact his droppings? I suddenly feel like I'm suffocating, and I fumble with the shelter's front flap and duck outside. Perhaps I come to my full height too quickly, for I'm just as suddenly dizzy. I stumble for the director's chair. My breaths are short and rapid as if I'd just climbed the canyon wall.

I walk the perimeter of my site to soak up the fresh air as snow crunches under my feet. I can't help but look for—and find— the tiny three-pronged tracks that circle the shelter. It's not just the tracks, though, that make me sick. It's where they lead.

I've become accustomed to simply squatting anywhere beyond the perimeter of my site whenever I feel the need to urinate, which at first struck me as crude but now seems as natural as the need itself. When it comes to solid waste, however, I've always gone to the same general area thirty feet beyond the slumped-over tent. It is here that the tracks lead. The ice and snow are scraped away to reveal—to reveal something that shouldn't be revealed once deposited, not ever, no matter how accustomed one might be to wilderness toilets. The tracks pick up after that, tinted deep brown.

I can't even imagine anything more unsanitary and obscene,

except the reality is even worse. That creature, that horrid, feces-tainted mouse slipped into my shelter last night and ripped the foil to shreds, depositing God only knows what kind of germs in the process. My stomach heaves but nothing comes out. I wish I could vomit. I wish I could expunge everything from my system that the mouse might have contaminated. I don't even have Clorox—or Lysol—nothing. How could I have thought when I swept the shelter floor with a dishtowel that I actually cleaned it? It isn't *clean.* It's covered in filth, not the kind of dirt you can see with the eyes, but the kind of foul that seeps through the skin and soils the very cells that make up the blood. I'd have to bathe in ammonia before I could feel clean.

Spirit or no spirit, it's me or the mouse, and I'll be damned if I won't kill it. One way or another. If I were to spot it just now I could twist off its head without a second thought.

DAY 17, NOVEMBER 27, DUSK

I dread the coming of another night, for *night* only means hour after hour waiting for light. I've hardly slept in three days. I've tried to maintain my routine: I wait until dawn to start the coffee and write in my journal, followed by brushing my teeth and washing my face. I still haven't dared to wash my hair again. Over half the water jugs are empty and I'm not yet halfway through my retreat even though it seems like I've been here forever.

I can't imagine twenty-three more days of this. In the afternoon I eat lunch and then gather firewood. I write more in my journal, stoke the fire in the wood stove, wash the dishes. I try to stay busy. I try not to think. I refuse to allow myself a nap, knowing that then I *really* couldn't sleep at night. But at the end of the day when I lay my head down, I don't sleep. I wait, listening for the tiny paws. I lay waiting and listening until dawn finally breaks and I can start the coffee again.

I still haven't caught the mouse.

I'm so tired that I feel like I'm someone else. It doesn't help that I am officially a criminal now that I've overstayed the legal limit on BLM land. I *feel* like a criminal holed up in some filthy rat hole, filthy because there is no way I can make it clean.

Perhaps it is true that the subconscious works out its quandaries in dreams, and without dreams one's mind begins to decay. There is a horrible darkness within me that I've never felt before. Perhaps it is true that when the body is deprived of sleep certain organs don't function, and the ability to convert sugars in the blood is impaired. Maybe that's why I don't feel like myself. I don't know if I ever will again, and I'm frightened of that because I don't even know what that means.

I lay on my sleeping bags, trying not to think of the mouse, but as the wind shrieks outside my shelter I think of the story I invented about the wicked witch who turned the giant into stone. The wind is her scornful laughter as she casts another spell and waves her wand over my desert canyon. *"Heeheeheeheehee!"* she cackles, and—*poof*—the mouse is a hundred times bigger. He's as big as my shelter, and now the witch waves her wand again and—*poof*—a dozen more giant mice rise from the ground. Deadly virus oozes from their mouths.

I can't take it. I can't take anymore. I've got to sleep. I can't keep my mind off the mouse. I can't keep my mind off time. Twenty-three more days. I can't make it. I'll go crazy.

Each day the darkness within me is worse. Each day it grows

stronger and stronger like a whirlpool sucking me deeper into a giant black pit. I fear the problem is even deeper than sleep deprivation. Perhaps it is as impossible to dictate how the mind reacts to long-term isolation as it is to control how the body reacts to severe cold. Hypothermia is the body's reaction. Arctic Madness is the mind's. As with hypothermia rational thought slowly slides into judgment failure, but the cause of Arctic Madness is mental deprivation rather than physical.

I don't know how much isolation the mind can take before it begins to break. Isolation is *punishment.* Prison guards know it. Torturers know it. There was no fate worse to the ancients than to be cast from the tribe. Even Thoreau went to town from time to time, perhaps nearly every day. In the absence of touch or conversation or any contact with someone else, the mind begins to doubt itself. The mind begins to turn against itself. Am I simply tired or am I beginning to lose my mind?

It's possible that what is happening to me is even more deep-seated than Arctic Madness. It's possible that it's even worse. It may be an inescapable part of Who I Am, passed from one generation to the next.

My mother hardly ever talked about her childhood. She came from a family of nine children—five girls, four boys—most of whom I met either before I could remember or not until I grew up, and so they weren't among the people I actively considered my relatives. All the girls' names ended in "iss." Lois, my mother, and then Phyllis, Janis, Alice, and Corliss. Mom says that all her mother had to do was yell "Iss!" and all five girls came running. That's about all I knew of Mom's childhood, except it seems that I've always known that my mother's dad died when she was about fifteen. I don't remember when I learned that he took his own life.

It wasn't until I was sixteen that I learned how my mother's father killed himself, and I might not have found out then except my mom got a phone call one summer night saying that her oldest sister, Alice, had done the same thing. Alice, like her father, had stuffed a rag in the muffler of the family car—she had two children—and sat inside with the windows rolled up until she died.

I never met Alice, and I still don't know what drove my mother's relatives to take their own lives. But for a long time I thought at least my dad's side of the family was normal. That's because I hadn't wondered about Grandpa Tony, my dad's grandfather—my grandpa's father, my great-grandfather. I only knew that he had died in his fifties. Maybe because I was so intrigued by this man I never knew, I named my son, Tony, after him. Only after my great-grandmother died—at ninety-four of natural causes—did even the slightest suspicion begin to cross my mind. I started asking questions. What did Grandpa Tony do for a living? A university professor. What were his hobbies? He was a voracious reader. He loved to scribble notes all over the pages. How did he die?

Finally, one day while Grandpa napped and my grandmother and I were alone in her living room, Grandma revealed the details in a whisper. Grandpa Tony shot himself. My great-grandmother found him with his head blown off. To spare her feelings, no one ever talked about it. Even my dad didn't know the whole truth.

I don't know what makes people take their own lives, but at some point they must suffer the greatest of defeats. Did my aunt or my grandfather or my great-grandfather enter the same darkness that now threatens me? Did they try to run from it, as I do now, desperate to return to the light? Was there a certain moment when they knew they couldn't return, so they let go and gave themselves up?

I don't know if my relatives had faith in their own souls. I don't know if I do, either, anymore. Maybe I was wrong all along. My soul hasn't exactly been spewing forth answers. It hasn't rushed to the rescue with my unique purpose in life. I've survived, but I'm starting to realize that survival isn't enough. I don't think it was enough for my relatives who took their own lives. Maybe what I'm looking for doesn't exist, no matter what I'm willing to do to find it. Even if it does, I'm not sure that I'm strong enough to stay here and search it out.

Chapter Fifteen

It frightens me that my hand shakes. I dip my brush into the bowl of paint and touch it to the canvas. My eyes squint in the sun's glare. I step back to judge my progress, unsure that what I mean to be a juniper tree looks like one. This morning I knew I had to get out of the shelter. Quit thinking for a while. Quit waiting for the mouse. Quit waiting for night, for the darkness to return.

The idea to paint my shelter isn't original. My grandmother—Dad's mom—once painted a life-size fish on her bathroom wall above the bathtub. Then she requested that each family member add his or her own to the wall, a kind of generational collage. I've always felt bad about mine because I was five years old and insisted on painting my fish all by myself. My mother tried to persuade me to wait a year or two, but Grandma took my side. All the other fish, painted by adults, looked like fish. My design—essentially, but not intentionally, a giant red whale with puckered lips—made minnows of the others.

I've ruled out painting fish on my shelter, but I'm not clear on what aspect of my desert environment to reflect. The fact that I can't sleep in this environment? The fact that I might contract a deadly virus from a mouse that lives in this environment? So I paint a juniper tree but I don't like how it looks. It's not the right color. I only brought a few paints: black, white, Alzarine Crimson Hue, Phthalocyanine Blue, Sundance Yellow, and Seabreeze Emerald—green, but not the same color green as a juniper tree. I've mixed in a little blue but it still doesn't look right.

Painting isn't helping. The darkness will come again, as surely as night.

Dip, brush. Dip, brush. Add a little blue. Dip, brush. Dip, brush.

Twenty-one more days.

Dip, brush.

Twenty-one more nights.

Just keep painting, that's the important thing, but I'm starting to shiver. My hand is trembling more by the minute. Dip, brush. Dip, brush.

The paint looks different than it did a moment ago. Little chunks of something now float in it. I dip the brush in the bowl and touch it to the canvas. The paint doesn't stick like it did before. It falls off, like little chunks of ice. I look again at the bowl. It *is* ice. The paint is freezing in the bowl.

I can't paint if the paint is frozen but I have to paint. I *must* paint. I will paint. I *will*.

I jab my brush into the bowl, scooping up little pieces of paint ice. I stab it on the canvas. The ice chunks fall to the ground. I stab at the canvas over and over until the paint freezes solid across the bottom of the bowl, but I stab on and on.

I stab the canvas as if I could slaughter my shelter. This place has turned me into a killer. I am enraged, furious at the cold, furious at the mouse, furious at every tree and rock and sage bush I see.

I let the brush fall to the ground, and suddenly the exhaustion is too much. I crawl inside the shelter and wrap my sleeping bags around me. If only I could sleep. God, how I long for rest, for peace. I pick up my journal and begin to write, fighting the darkness with all I have left, a tired army born of thoughts and feelings somewhere deep inside my soul.

The shelter starts to spin and the paper blurs. I feel like I'm falling, surrounded by a multitude of sinewy forms. I know, having listened to my grandfather and then my father read *A Christmas Carol* each year of my life, that they are ghosts. They moan, eerie regrets of broken hearts, unfulfilled dreams, wasted lives. Above the moans my grandfather's voice reads Marley's explanation of their presence to Scrooge:

> *It is required of every man that the spirit within him should walk abroad among his fellow-men, and travel far and wide; and if that spirit goes not forth in life, it is condemned to do so after death. It is doomed to wander through the world—oh, woe is me!—and witness what it cannot share, but might have shared on earth, and turned to happiness!*

I see now as if I am looking through Scrooge's own eyes as Marley's ghost backed away toward the window; with every step Marley took, the window opened more and Scrooge looked out into the night.

The air filled with phantoms, wandering hither and thither in restless haste, and moaning as they went. Every one of them wore chains like Marley's Ghost . . . the misery with them all was, clearly, that they sought to interfere, for good, in human matters, and had lost the power for ever.

I am horrified by these ghosts, for just as Scrooge went on to be haunted by three more Christmas ghosts, so I perceive that I will soon meet the spirits of my three relatives who took their own lives. They will come not with words of wisdom and gentle truth, but with anguish and sorrow and bitter remorse. They will tell me that it is too late to escape the darkness. They will float around my shelter and I'm afraid of what they'll look like. I don't want to see them but I can't close my eyes because they will come. Then I do see them, filling the shelter as it swells like a balloon about to explode.

I sit straight up in my sleeping bags. Sweat drips off my forehead. A dream, but I don't believe it. A *dream,* that's all. *Sleep,* at last. But now I know I won't sleep again. Not here, for the ghosts await me. It frightens me that part of my mind thinks those ghosts are real, and frightens me even more that perhaps they are. To have faced death during the blizzard was fear of one kind. To face my own mind, unprotected by its normal defenses, is absolute terror. Now I know I can't do it.

I shove the sleeping bag aside and throw open the shelter's flap door, grabbing my Reeboks as I duck outside. My feet feel the instant pain of the snow. I hop to the director's chair and put my shoes on. My breaths are short and rapid, and I simply stand there, looking out of the canyon to the white desert floor below.

I can't stay here. I was wrong. Wrong about everything.

The sun has almost completed its daily path across the sky. In an hour or so it will dip behind the mountains to the west, and dusk will begin. There isn't enough time to hike to the road—not to mention to the wildlife refuge—before dark. I dread walking twenty-five miles through the desert wilderness, even during the day, but I can't take it anymore. I've got to get out of here but I can't, not tonight. Tomorrow. I only hope it's soon enough.

In nineteen days I've learned a new set of rules, rules that are totally foreign to the world beyond the desert, rules that Man, insulated in his electric cities, has long since forgotten. Night is falling, and the creatures of the day must make way for the creatures of the dark who have slumbered through daylight in their burrows of cold rock and dirt. Their intuitions will soon wake them, and I, like all other creatures of the day, must make way. But I am desperate for a campfire, and not just the meager flames the firewood I gathered and stomped for the woodstove would provide. Tonight of all nights I do not wish to huddle in my shelter waiting for the mouse, though I hold little hope of finding wood not soaked by the snow.

I pick up my ax, sensing the eyes of some creature of the night already awakened, already upon me, lurking in the shadows, watching my every move. If only they'll leave me alone one more night, this canyon will belong to only them again.

I follow a wash toward the back of the canyon, so weary that I hardly notice my footsteps until I spot a juniper tree just ahead. I'm sure I haven't seen it before. I turn around trying to get my bearings. I *always* stay within sight of my shelter, but now I don't see it. I can't have come that far, but there's Pisa Rock, back behind me, silhouetted black against the darkening sky. I've never seen it from this angle.

The junipers near my site are spindly and sparse, standing not much taller than my head. This tree towers fifteen feet into the sky, however, and its lush, green branches, loaded with silver-blue berries, hang nearly to the ground. This tree, compared with the others in the canyon, not only survives its harsh life but thrives. If every tree in the canyon looked like this the desert would transform into a forest, but as it is, this juniper alone lives its potential. Why? All the trees reside in the same soil. All the trees receive the same meager dose of rainfall. Does this tree simply benefit from better genes than the others? Do the other trees feel unequal?

I spread the tree's limbs aside and duck between them, closing my eyes against the sharp needles that snag my knit cap. Dry twigs snap against my cheek. The trunk is even bolder than I imagined, nearly two feet in diameter with long, stringy sheets of bark. But it isn't the bark that catches my attention. On the ground beside the trunk, untouched from snow, protected from above by a perfect canopy of branches, is something else. Perhaps I am especially now a poor judge of what distinguishes the wondrous from the mundane, but to my eyes the sight is nothing short of a miracle: firewood. Dry firewood. Enough for a bonfire. It'll take three trips at least—two of the fallen limbs are six feet long and a foot wide. I don't know if I can get them back to my site before dark. If only I could stop the night.

My arm aches as I hug a load of the smaller branches to my chest. The ax is now my walking staff as I pick carefully across the snowy ground. I feel, once again, the eyes of some hidden creature watching me and I urge myself faster.

Finally, seeing the back of my shelter, I pick up the pace. The sky is indigo and a star or perhaps a planet twinkles white. Only the horizon is lit, the clouds over the mountains glow angry orange and red in the day's final struggle. Dark is but minutes away. I'm not sure I can beat it if I return for the large limbs. But I must. An armload of wood is nothing against the night.

The beam of my propane lantern grows smaller as I stumble back up the wash along the path that my footprints have packed into the snow.

The juniper is as sinewy as one of the phantoms in my dream against the background of snow, still slightly tinged by the sunset. I pull the first limb from under the branches, and then the second, but I'll have to leave the ax here. I heave one bough under the crook of my arm, and stoop to pick up the other. The lantern back at my site flickers like a single candle. I keep my eyes upon it. It's slow going, and the limbs dragging on the ground frame my footprints with parallel lines in the snow. Onward I walk toward the light, my feet crunching in harmony with the limbs' rhythmic bounces across exposed stones.

I've never been so grateful to return to my site. Even the creatures of the night can't touch me as long as a fire burns bright. I toss a few dry sagebrushes into the firepit with a crumpled newspaper and add the smallest of the limbs before striking a match. The spark catches the newspaper and at once the air is filled with the hiss and pops of scorching sage.

The firepit now dances with flames, casting long shadows beyond my site. If I dared to look I'd see the glowing amber eyes of a giant mouse, eight feet tall with teeth so big they could tear through my neck in one giant bite.

Stop it, I tell myself. I add more branches and the flames leap higher.

It's out there, and it's going to eat me.

Stop it.

I pull the director's chair close to the firepit and wrap my jacket tight around my chest. My cheeks flush in the heat. I stare into the flames and squint. White. Yellow. Orange. Red. Black. A blur of distinct lines and hues. A memory seems to float forward in my mind as if carried in the smoke. Other lights, other colors. A time long past; a time when I felt safe and warm, curled up in my grandparents' living room squinting into the lights of the Christmas tree while Grandpa read *A Christmas Carol.* Marley's ghost didn't scare me. Nothing could hurt me as long as the lights blinked so pretty on the tree.

But now I am in danger, fearing my own mind the most. In the past few days I've gradually lost touch with reality, not in a continuous downhill slide but in periodic bouts from which I suddenly recover, aware that I've been momentarily nuts, aware that it could and probably will happen again. It's too much. Even if my sanity weren't in jeopardy, it is useless to stay. I did not come here intending to fixate on a mouse, but now I'm helpless to stop it. My mind has chosen that creature to represent all my fears; I'm not capable of overcoming them all lumped together as one.

The campfire slowly fades into coals, and I toss on another log that lands in the pit with a shower of sparks, crackling like a mountain waterfall cascading into a ravine. If there were any other sounds in the night, perhaps I wouldn't notice the subtle hiss when an errant spark flies beyond the firepit and extinguishes into nothing. It is not so much a hiss as a sigh.

If there were any other sounds in the night, perhaps I wouldn't hear my own breaths, but it is so quiet that my heartbeat makes an audible *pabump, pabump.*

If there were any other sounds in the night, any at all—the chirping of crickets or the croaking of frogs, a rustling in the leaves or a babbling in a brook; if there was even a single reverberation of even a single pebble bouncing down the cliffs or if any creature scurried among the sage; indeed, it must be very quiet before one hears one's own heartbeat, but if there were any other sounds in the night than that, I am certain I could not hear what I do now.

A long, low note. A musical note, as if played by a pipe organ in a church. The first is followed by another long note a third of the scale higher, and then five more notes follow that, and then the melody repeats over. At first I wonder if it's just my imagination, but then the Squirrel Man's forewarning echoes in my mind. *You're lucky if you hear it,* he said, *because that means your ears have learned to work again.*

My ears have never heard anything like this. It is at once joyous and mournful, in one breath both hope and despair, heavenly but of the earth, as if the human voice is not alone in its ability to express the very contents of its soul. The sound could fill a cathedral, yet a disturbance as subtle as a sigh sends it fleeing back into the coals.

I can't explain why I've never heard this before, but I suppose the circumstances must be exactly right. Silence, of course, but perhaps a moment of silence isn't enough. It could be that it's only audible in the desert and only when the humidity and temperature are exactly so. The conditions might be so specific that if any of a hundred variables aren't precisely right there is no music, or perhaps the Squirrel Man was right. Maybe the music can always be heard if the ears know how to listen.

The sound is so wondrous that, for a few moments, I almost find courage against the darkness. But as the logs burn down, as the flames flicker lower and lower, I watch a single flame flare only four inches into the air in one last desperate attempt to reach the sky before it collapses, spent, leaving the darkness to edge closer. I am that flame. I too am spent. Even the fire's music isn't enough to save me now.

I wish I could ask my aunt and my mom's father and my great-grandfather what they once lived for. I wish I could ask them why they gave up, why they abandoned their dreams. Perhaps that is suicide's most subtle form. Perhaps once the first dream is left to die it's easier to leave the next and the next until they're all gone. It frightens me that tomorrow I will abandon a dream. It horrifies me that I have no more to abandon.

If I retire to my shelter while the last coals still glow, maybe the light will help me not be so afraid. I tuck myself into the sleeping bags and pick up my journal. I'm surprised to find that the page following this morning's entry is already full of words. Of course— this afternoon, before I drifted off to dream of the ghosts. I hardly remember writing. Curious, I read the entry. And then I read it again.

I set the journal down, take a sip of water, light a cigarette and pick up the journal again. I read the entry a third time. And I still don't get it.

Let us consider the darkness inside you. You are frightened that it will consume you, pulling you into a hole from which there is no return. Truly it may, but only because you allow it.

Do you really believe the darkness has a power of its own to destroy you? That would be possible only if it were separate from you. The darkness is no more separate from you than I am, though you perceive me as a voice separate from your own.

Let us consider power. Power simply is. It is within you—where else could it go? When one part of you denies its power, another part of you must accept it. The less powerful you believe yourself to be, the more power is given to the darkness. And then you don't believe that the power remains within you, but it does.

Have you considered every possible way to deal with the mouse? You say you are powerless to catch it, and the darkness grows greater.

Have you considered every possible way to deal with time, or have you assumed that lacking a way to make it pass faster, you are conquered by an enemy? You have made yourself a victim to time and thus the darkness consumes you.

Why would you wish time to pass faster? Twenty-one days stretch before you as an eternity. As if twenty-one days could possibly be enough!

You say that you have not found the answers to your questions, but perhaps you have not spent your days wisely. You think you can simply allow time to pass while you wait for answers to fall from the sky. Not so.

You came to the desert to unravel the mystery of what you should do with your life, and yet you have not addressed what you should do with forty days. Do not mistake them as separate questions. Remember that the power within you cannot be lost. The darkness cannot be escaped except by facing it.

ᴪ

I take a long puff on my cigarette, stub it out and then light another. Smoke curls above my head to disperse in a haze with the candle's smoke. I read the entry again, words that address "me" as "you." Crazy people talk to themselves, perhaps they also write to themselves. Crazy people don't even know they're crazy, just like hypothermia victims don't know they're cold. Their minds trick them into stripping off their clothes to lay in the snow, their last desperate act before they succumb. Maybe at first you suspect you're in trouble, but then you lose complete touch with reality.

I'm still perplexed that I can't remember writing those words. They don't *sound* crazy, exactly, except they don't seem to be mine. *The darkness is no more separate from you than I am, though you perceive me as a voice separate from your own.* I don't understand. Why would I question whether I've considered every way of dealing with the mouse when I know that I have? The trap doesn't work. There's no way to seal the shelter more tightly.

I've done my best to deal with time. I don't know what *perhaps you have not spent your days wisely* means. I don't think I would have done anything differently even if I were the last person on earth, but now a shiver tingles down my spine. If I were the last person on earth and things got tough, I couldn't just leave. If the darkness overtook my mind, I couldn't simply hike out the next day.

But that's not a fair comparison. I'm not the last person on earth. I'm a mother, a daughter, a sister. I don't exist in a vacuum. My actions affect others, even here. What I do matters to someone besides myself.

But what if I really was the last person on earth? When I was a kid, we lived fifteen miles from Fort Lewis Army Base and McChord Air Force Base, and those were the days of Vietnam and the Cold War. Kids at school used to taunt each other that with so much military power in our area we'd probably be among the first to be "taken out" by the Commies. Sometimes at night I'd hear the jets roar through the sky, and I'd wonder if they were ours or theirs. I'd wonder if the Big One was about to blow.

My worst fear was that everybody perished in the attack except me, and I had to figure out how to live on my own. There'd be plenty of food in the grocery stores. The only thing I knew how to cook, however, were frozen dinners and boxed macaroni and cheese, and I supposed electricity would be in short supply. I tried to calculate how long frozen dinners would stay frozen if the freezers quit working. I thought I could live a long time on potato chips and Cheese Whiz.

I would find everything I needed at the mall—free, of course, because there wouldn't be anyone to pay. I have to admit that the notion of all the toys I could ever want appealed to me. I'd get my clothes from the best department store, not hand-me-downs from my older cousins, not at the Goodwill Thrift Store where my mother made us shop. I could have anything my heart desired. The only problem was that then I'd think about how much I'd miss my parents and my sisters and my grandparents and my friends, and I'd become so sad and frightened that not even the fantasy of all the toys in the world made me feel better. I never got far enough into the nuclear holocaust scenario to figure out the purpose of my life.

Surely, surely if I were the last person on earth, I wouldn't allow myself to languish into nothingness. I would find something to do. I would find something to look forward to. I'd think of something *fun,* even though I've outgrown toy stores. That's probably why, for the past eighteen days, I've mostly stayed in bed. It's not as if the desert is a laugh a minute. It's not a lot of fun to hold up a tent through a blizzard. It's not a lot of fun to wake up with a mouse on your head. It's not a lot of fun to wonder whether you're losing your mind. Still, if I had to be here the rest of my life I'd probably manage to find some iota of pleasure in my existence.

Even here in this desert canyon I've found occasions to celebrate. Surviving the blizzard. The arrival of the wood stove. Eating pumpkin and olives on Thanksgiving with Felipe. Compared with the rest of the days, those were practically orgies of merriment. But maybe I could have made the other days more fun if I'd really worked at it. I wish I had. It might have made a difference. I didn't realize just how important fun is. Now I'd have to say that it too belongs on Mrs. Darling's list of life's essentials.

I didn't even make it to the halfway mark. I couldn't even hack it for twenty days. It's not really my fault. I came here unprepared for what I might experience. It wasn't fair to jeopardize my son's happiness and welfare by risking my life. He'll be so relieved to hear my voice tomorrow. I'll tell him he'll never have to worry about me doing anything dangerous again.

It probably won't occur to him for many years that his mother failed at what she set out to accomplish. Someday he'll realize I gave up, and maybe that will make him determined never to give up himself. But maybe instead he'll use my failure to justify his own, just as I have used the defeat of my relatives to warrant mine.

What if my aunt had tried to last just one more night? What if my mother's father had delayed his surrender twenty-four hours more? What if my great-grandfather had somehow found the strength to put down the gun and walk away, knowing he could always pick it up again tomorrow?

What if I could find the strength to persevere?

If I could just make it to the halfway point, if I could just make it twenty days, maybe, *maybe* something would be different. Tonight I heard music in the fire—I *heard* it. I wonder what else exists that the ears could hear if the circumstances were just right. I don't know if I'm just grasping at straws. For all I do know, I've already failed. Two more days means two more nights, and I don't know how I can stand the nights. I don't know how to face the darkness. But if I could just find a way to hold on two more days, maybe, *maybe* I would still have a chance.

Chapter Sixteen

When I open my eyes, I almost can't believe it's true. Today is Day 20.

Somehow I made it. I feel like Scrooge who, waking from his encounter with Marley and the Ghosts of Christmases Past, Present and Future, discovers that it is not too late to change his fate. It is not too late for me. Somehow I pushed through the darkness, at least for now, and on the other side is hope.

Perhaps it is innate to the human spirit that upon reaching the halfway mark of any endeavor, the definition of what's possible alters to include reaching the finish. Perhaps a buoyant swell of optimism is nature's reward for keeping one's own head above water long enough to find a wave to ride to shore. If I just hang on a little longer, surely I will find that wave. Indeed, on this day I have cause to celebrate.

As I lay in my sleeping bags waiting for the coffee to perk, it occurs to me that perhaps I really could celebrate. This day really could be different from the others. If I tried it could even be fun and—and this thought sends a tingle of pleasure through each vein in my body—I'll even wash my hair. Yes, and I'll have a giant campfire, the biggest and best this canyon has ever seen, and—man, I'm really rolling now—I'll make fry-bread and see if I can rustle up Felipe for some company. We'll make a party of it.

I rise from my sleeping bags with a playfulness I'd almost forgotten I possess. A party in the desert—now that's rich. My guest of honor is a fly. I do hope he'll come. Nothing ruins a party like no-shows. I should know. I was almost one myself.

The sun is directly above my head by the time I finish collecting firewood. When I retrieved my ax under the towering juniper, I discovered a dead tree just beyond it, its branches bleached gray and totally without needles. The pile of wood now stacked by the firepit could support the stove for a week if it were busted to size but I'm pulling out all the stops, and if I burn all the giant limbs tonight that's just fine. The higher the flames, the smaller the darkness. Tomorrow I'll conserve, today I'll splurge.

Tomorrow. Two days ago I could hardly imagine a tomorrow.

It's been twenty days since Bret and Dana lit the first fire in what's become my firepit. Sticks and sagebrush on bare ground, that's how it all started. Now when I shovel out the accumulated ashes, the pit is nearly two feet deep and four across. I couldn't have dug it in the frozen ground; the fires over the past twenty days have accomplished that for me. Even still, it looks more like a hole in the ground than a true firepit, and I decide to dress it up in a manner worthy of a primal party.

Because stones are scattered liberally across the canyon, the only limitation is my ability to transport them. I never realized how heavy rocks are, probably because I've never gone out of my way to move them, and I've never felt the sense of accomplishment at actually doing so. It's quite a thrill, really, to throw my body weight at odds with stone. Stones any bigger than basketballs beat me without much of a contest, but I conclude that basketball size is sufficient anyway.

After gathering about fifty rocks, I dig a shallow trench around the pit as a foundation. I heave the stones into place, one after another until the pit is completely ringed, and then I start with the second layer. On the side that my fire could be seen from the valley I add not only a third level but a fourth. Between the two foot depth of the pit itself and the nearly three-foot stone wall, I doubt that more than just a subtle glow from the fire could now be seen from the valley below.

More sophisticated eyes might not agree, but to mine the result is nothing short of an architectural wonder. It's an actual *structure* for fire, a cathedral meritorious of the music contained in the flames. The structure could last forever—forever—and there's no real reason it won't. I've never before built something that could be discovered a thousand or five thousand or ten thousand years from now.

Something wondrous is happening within me. Since I've begun to consider what I'd do if I were the last person on earth, I'm beginning to realize things I've never known about myself. If I were the last person on earth, I would try to build something that could last forever so that some small piece of *me* would last forever. Somehow this seems important. Somehow this seems to be an element of purpose in its purest form. Perhaps it is only a tiny ingredient, but I can't help but dare to believe that maybe, *maybe* the pieces might finally be beginning to come together.

It's warm enough today that I'm in high hopes that Felipe will make an appearance. I decide to cook the fry-bread to encourage him while there's still time for the rodent-enticing odors to dissipate. I haven't used any oil since I fried the first batch on Thanksgiving, and it takes me a moment to remember that I stowed the bottle in the dilapidated tent. Naturally, it rolled to the very back corner, and I'm obliged to remove most of the boxes and bags and about fifteen empty water jugs and crawl in on my stomach just to get to it.

The effort may have been for nothing. Instead of being honey colored and clear, the oil is murky muck. It looks like the grease Mom kept in an old gallon pickle jar in the pantry. Whenever she fried meat she'd pour the drippings into the jar—for what eventual purpose, I never dared ask, but I hoped it was automotive rather than culinary. Mother and her grease. I haven't thought about that in ages.

When I was fourteen my mom cooked for our church's summer camp. We kids expected bacon and sausage every morning, and every morning Mom poured the drippings into a coffee can to cool because even at camp she saved the grease. Each day the reservoir got deeper and deeper, gooier and gooier.

One afternoon, an hour or so before dinner while we campers played volleyball, the sound of a piercing shriek brought our game to an immediate halt. We ran to the kitchen and crowded between the refrigerators and ovens to find my mother doubled over, half-wheezing, half-laughing. I pushed through the campers to reach her side. "What happened?"

She picked up the coffee can and tipped it down for all to view. There, swimming as madly as his little legs would move in the nearly hardened fat, was a mouse. Mom had been about to pour sizzling hamburger grease right on its head when she spotted it. My mother endured too many of Dad's mouse projects to actually be afraid of the little guy, but it startled her half to death.

His fate was certain, no doubt about it. Mom slipped into plastic gloves and tried to wipe the ooze off his fur, but he wasn't as willing a patient as the otter had been. Finally she just dumped him in the yard. We prayed for him, sort of, but we figured that was one time when prayer probably wouldn't cheat a cat.

Perhaps the answer to my mouse problem is right here in this bottle. Vegetable oil isn't bacon grease but the consistency is nearly identical, probably because of the cold. It's definitely gooey. If a mouse got in I doubt it could get out. All I have to do is figure out how to convince Little Sport to take a dive.

After transferring my coffee grounds to a Ziploc bag I've got an empty coffee can, step one. I dump the oil in, step two. Step three is already in the works. Fry-bread. The perfect bait. The most obvious spot for the contraption is behind my shelter, where I've found the highest concentration of tracks. I crumble up some fry-bread around the coffee can and sprinkle crumbs onto the oil's surface. Hopefully the mouse will be so tempted from his first taste that he'll jump in for his last, but I don't know. Little Sport has proven himself reasonably intelligent thus far. He's avoided the pan-on-a-fork trap for over a week.

But if this works it'll catch him before he ever enters the shelter, and that *really* makes this a special day. How odd that I didn't think of my mom's grease before, and how strange that the journal entry questioned whether I had considered every possibility for dealing with the mouse. I thought I had. Makes me wonder what other possibilities I haven't considered for problems bigger than mice.

❦

The sun, sinking toward the western horizon, beckons me to finish my preparations in haste. As I duck inside the shelter, a flash on the wall catches my eye. I didn't realize when I painted the juniper tree on the outside that I'd be able to see it from the inside as well. I assumed the fabric was relatively nontransparent. Instead, the tree glows like a stained-glass window, lit from behind by the sun, sparkling and green in contrast to its duller tan background. The effect is so cheering that it makes me wish I had painted more figures before the paint froze.

I wash the dishes, straighten my bedding, put the hatchet under the pillow and ready the tiny bedside table with its candle, glass of water—maybe tonight it won't freeze—and matches. The hand towel once again serves as my mop. I have no illusions that I've sanitized the floor but at least the top layer of dirt is gone. Now comes the moment I've been waiting for.

The wood stove, stoked to the hilt, soon warms the shelter enough that I remove my sweater and ski pants and then my thermal shirt and stirrup pants. I haven't seen my legs in ten days. I'm shocked at the mass of black and yellowish bruises stretching nearly solid from my knees to my ankles. It's hard to crawl in and out of the shelter without banging my legs on the doorstop. It hurts every time, but I hadn't realized the extent of the battering. It's not just the bruises. My skin is so dry that it falls in flakes at the slightest touch. The insides of my pant-legs are coated white with dead skin. In my entire adult life I've never gone twenty days without shaving my legs. Spindly hairs stick straight up from my calves half an inch long. I long for the razor I didn't bring, though at this point a lawn mower might be more appropriate.

I've *missed* feeling like a woman. I can't imagine that a man would spend twenty days in the desert and then complain, "I've only had two baths in twenty days. I just don't feel masculine anymore." After the first ten days I felt like a goddess when I washed my hair, but that feeling didn't last long. The last ten days have taken an even heavier toll on my sense of femininity. I *miss* the frills. I could go for a little lipstick, a pale pink negligee, a bit of lace here and there. I've slept in a sleeping bag so long that I can't even remember what sheets feel like, much less silk pillow cases. What I'd give for a dab of perfume, a long-stem rose and a powder puff. I wouldn't want my entire identity as a woman to rest on the availability of such items, but I'd be lying if I said I'd outgrown them here in the desert. I'd be an even bigger liar to say I wanted to.

I can't claim to feel like a goddess, but after scrubbing my scalp and rinsing it twice, I do feel—and smell—more like a member of my gender. It feels even better to smooth lotion over my legs. The real stunner, however, is a discovery I make while scavenging on the shelf for the lotion. Somehow a bottle of fingernail polish slipped into my toiletries. I didn't intentionally bring it, and I don't remember seeing it before, but here it is. My favorite color. Lollipop pink.

I'm surprised my nails have held up so well. Gathering firewood isn't easy on the hands, and the tips of my gloves have now worn completely through. None of my nails have broken or cracked, but they're stained gray with wood sap and ashes. As I touch the brush to each nail, it amazes me how a little color can transform even the blandest medium, just as the juniper painted on the shelter gives it a touch of delight.

It's only with the greatest reluctance that I slip my legs back into the stirrup pants. I shake the dead skin flakes out the shelter door but still feel a moment's regret that my party attire is no more lavish than this. Never mind. My hair is clean, and Felipe won't care, except I haven't seen any sign of Felipe. Maybe he's not coming. If I remember correctly, my dad once said that flies only live about three days. After he studied mice he researched fruit flies. At least he didn't keep them in my bedroom, although Mom might have preferred that to the jars of rotting bananas and or-anges Dad put all over the kitchen to attract the flies.

I might have to be my own guest of honor.

If that's the case, I really can't go to the party looking so drab. Then I have an idea. I duck out of the shelter with a bowl and return a few moments later with a supply of fresh juniper berries. In my Girl Scout days I learned that no first-aid kit is complete without a needle to remove slivers, and fortunately I included one with a big enough eye to accept a length of dental floss. I hold my breath, not sure that the silver-black berries won't deteriorate when I stab them with the needle, but they don't. Before long I've got a strand eighteen inches long, and when I tie the ends together I've got a necklace. Lollipop-pink nails, clean hair, and jewelry to boot. I pronounce myself the very model of desert chic.

In the entire existence of this canyon, there could never have been a more beautiful sunset than tonight's. If I were to spill every bottle of nail polish I've ever owned—including the blue and gold I wore in high school in honor of our team colors—and if they swirled and twirled and mingled and mixed and swooshed all together, the result still couldn't rival the shades cresting over the moun-tains to the west. Pink, red, orange; cranberry, mauve, peach;

plum, crimson, apricot; violet, blue, purple. There is not one hue missing.

With every passing moment the colors deepen as if an artist were blending black into the mixture one drop at a time. I wish the sky would resist and hold itself exactly as it is for all time, but as the stars begin to appear I realize the shortsightedness of that wish. The heavens transform before my eyes into a Christmas light show furnished by Nature itself. Even the campfire contributes, spewing a shower of glimmering sparks twelve feet into the air.

The stars remind me of when I was six years old and my uncle visited us at our house on Christmas Eve, one of the few Christmases we didn't all travel to my grandparents' in California. When Dad answered the door, my uncle practically blew right past him.

"Where's Debi?" he shouted. "Where is she? Did she see it?"

"What?" I cried, running up to him. "See *what?*"

"You mean you didn't?" my uncle said. He shook his head side to side. "That's too bad. I'm sure he's gone now."

"Who's gone?" I asked.

"Oh, never mind," my uncle said. "It's too late to see him now."

"Who, Uncle?" I tugged at his pants.

"Santa Claus," he said. "I saw him and his sleigh flying in the sky just now—right above your house—him and his eight tiny reindeer. I'm surprised you didn't hear the bells—"

I dashed outside and craned my neck to scan the whole sky, praying that it wasn't too late. The stars were just as they are tonight, so bright that I couldn't tell which of the billion blinking lights might actually be eight tiny reindeer. Any of them, none of them. My ears strained to at least hear the bells, but it was too late even for that.

"Maybe next year," my uncle said, joining me in the yard. I thought the sparkle in his eye was just a reflection of the stars.

I saw Mommy kissing Santa Claus underneath the mistletoe last night.
   She didn't see me creep down the stairs to take a peek.
   She thought that I was upstairs in my bedroom fast asleep.
   Without a pause I throw another log on the fire.
   Then I saw Mommy tickle Santa Claus, underneath his beard so snowy white.
   I pick up the pace and sing at the top of my lungs:
   What a laugh it would have been if Daddy had only seen
   Mommy kissing Santa Claus, Last Night!

I've now sung all the Christmas carols I know. Starting with *Jingle Bells,* I ran the whole repertoire. *O Little Town of Bethlehem, Silver Bells*—even though I don't know all the words—*I'm Dreaming of a White Christmas, Chestnuts Roasting on an Open Fire, We Three Kings*—not bad entertainment on a cold desert night. I even got a laugh out of imagining Mommy kissing Santa Claus in front of their poor kid.

I tip back my head, remembering when I was six, remembering when I believed that Santa was real. The Christmas after my uncle visited us, my family once again gathered in my grandparents' living room for the reading of *A Christmas Carol.* When Grandpa finished, I pleaded to go outside and wait for a glimpse of Santa and his sleigh.

"I could show you something even better," my grandpa said.

"There *isn't* anything better," I said.

"All right," he said. "Maybe when you're older—" and that's all he had to say.

"I'm old enough now."

Grandpa bundled me up and tucked me in the car, and we drove for so long that I wondered if he was taking me clear to the North Pole. When he turned off the main street and told me to look, I thought he actually had.

"Where *are* we?" I asked.

"This is Candy Cane Lane."

He was right. It was even better than seeing Santa and his reindeer in the sky. Grandpa had brought me to a neighborhood of absolute magic. Each house was completely aglow in color, lights strung from the eaves, blinking on every window and flashing on every tree. Some of the yards dazzled my eyes with brightly painted wooden scenes: Santas, elves, reindeer—even a crèche, complete with wooden donkeys. But the yard I remember most had a giant four-poster bed, right in the middle of the lawn. A spotlight shone on the bed where the chests of an animated Ma and Pa rose and fell with their snores. But that wasn't the best part. Another spotlight shone on an electric train track that ran under and around the bed. Two engines, disguised as a cat and a mouse, chased each other around the track in a never-ending race.

"Pull over, Grandpa," I begged, but we weren't the only ones who had come to Candy Cane Lane. The line of traffic behind us was too thick. I began to cry.

"What's this?" Grandpa said. "Crying on Christmas Eve?"

"But I want to see it," I wailed. "It'll never be the same again." I strained for another look, but saw only the headlights of the car behind us. "Please, Grandpa."

He didn't say a word. He just kept driving, pointing out the beautiful lights on other houses. I hardly saw them through my tears. And then he swung into a driveway. "Maybe they won't mind, just for a minute," he said. "Come on, then, let's go back for a look."

I couldn't believe my ears, but the next minute Grandpa took my hand and we walked back to the yard where the cat and mouse chased each other around the bed. "Isn't it wonderful?" I asked my grandfather.

"It is at that," Grandpa said. We stood there a long time, he and I. I don't know what he was thinking, but I remember my thoughts exactly. I was dreaming that when I grew up I was going to create the most magical Christmas scene in the world.

I'm disappointed when the last of the logs settle into coals. The party is nearly over. Tomorrow it's back to the real desert. Twenty days of my retreat still stretch before me, and more than anything I want to make it to the finish. I still wonder how I will cope with the time. Every day can't be a party, and I fear the darkness will return. I don't know how I could face it again, so I must try to stave it off before its threat becomes a promise.

If I have learned anything from these first twenty days it's that human nature does not tolerate inactivity well. As a child when I complained, "there's nothing to do," my mother said she'd be happy to help. Her options generally included vacuuming the living room or washing the kitchen windows or brushing spider webs off the ceiling, and typically I concluded that there *was* something to do, something very important and sorry, I'd have to vacuum later. I found something to do. I invented something to do. I, like most children, could entertain myself if pressed to do so.

Perhaps as an adult I've allowed that skill to go lax. In the absence of others and in the absence of external stimuli I've practically gone nuts. The notion of spending the next twenty days similarly nonengaged is truly repulsive. I've learned the cost.

But tonight I entertained myself without even the company of a fly. Just me, just my songs, just my memories, just as if I really were the last person on earth. I'm beginning to think that perhaps the soul doesn't spew forth its answers, but instead floats them in glass buoys from the deepest regions of the heart. Tonight I've realized that if I were the last person on earth, I would still celebrate Christmas. I would read *A Christmas Carol* out loud. I would sing every Christmas song whether I could remember all the words or not. I would decorate my house and I would hang ornaments on a tree.

I would keep Christmas because it is humanity in its best dress. It is an uncle teasing a niece, a grandfather indulging a granddaughter, a father's uproarious laughter. It is patience in long lines, tolerance in busy streets. It the consideration of others' happiness and the grateful acceptance of their kind wishes. It is the appreciation of beauty and the rekindling of hope. To quote my father's favorite description in *A Christmas Carol,* it is, quite simply, "apoplectic opulence."

Each time Dad gets to that phrase he looks up from the book to explain, for the benefit of us who've only heard the story thirty times instead of his fifty, that *apoplectic* is the state of being highly excited, and *opulence* means abundance. Highly excited abundance. Dickens was referring to a profusion of pot-bellied baskets spilling chestnuts from grocers' doors out onto the streets, but I like to believe that at Christmas there's a bit of apoplectic opulence in us all. If I were the last person on earth, I would dig deep in my heart to find it.

And yet, now that my songs have faded into the night, here in my canyon there is not one sign that Christmas is coming, not one bit of evidence that Christmas even exists. There are no decorations, no ornaments, no garlands or bows. If I would keep Christmas as the last person on earth, surely I would keep it before such an eventuality. Maybe it's not to late to fulfill my childhood dream, to create the most magical Christmas scene in the . . . well, perhaps it's not important to create the most magical scene in the world. I suspect it's important to create whatever little bit of magic I can muster.

Chapter Seventeen

It's not going to be easy, I decide as I crouch on my knees to examine my shelter from a different perspective, but it might work. It's not like I can hang shiny ornaments and tinsel from every tree. I can't string blinking lights from every cliff. I don't have an animated Ma and Pa, much less a four-poster bed. Candy Cane Lane this canyon will never be. But the idea might just work.

I circle the shelter, pausing to peer into the can of oil at the rear. I'd feel guilty if I killed a mouse, but I'm still disappointed not to find one floating in the thick oil, although each and every crumb of fry-bread bait is gone. Last night I slept better, two and three hours at a time. Sometimes a little hope goes a long way, but not once the hope proves false. The problem could be that the rim of the can is too high off the ground. From the mouse's viewpoint the coffee can must be the equivalent of five stories high. Maybe a ramp up to edge would help persuade the rogue to explore a little further, so I find a ten-inch stick and lean it against the can. To-night I'll rebait the whole contraption, including the ramp, right up to the rim. It's worth a try.

And so is the shelter. I continue ambling, sometimes stand-ing on my tiptoes to gauge whether my hand can reach the center beam, sometimes folding an errant corner of canvas out of the way, until I reach the front again and take fifteen paces forward and turn around for an overall view. Certainly I didn't plan the shape of the shelter for this purpose, and it's a bit of a stretch to imagine the finished design, but still, it just might work.

Not that I've ever made a gingerbread house before, much less a life-size version. In fifth grade I once used powdered-sugar icing to glue four graham cracker halves into a box and propped two more halves on top for the roof and then smothered the whole thing with gumdrops, but I don't think that counts. It would have collapsed after thirty seconds even if I hadn't eaten it first. When my sisters were thirteen, they attempted to make the genuine ar-ticle to give as their Christmas gift to Grandma. The gingerbread turned out too thick, though, and no matter how much icing they used the walls wouldn't stay together. Or maybe the icing was too thin, because the candies wouldn't stay on either. If it had been my project, I would have eaten the disaster and called it a day, but my sisters tried and tried and baked batch after batch of ginger-bread until they got it right. Fifteen years later my grandmother still pulls it out of storage for her Christmas centerpiece.

Actually, my shelter only resembles the roof portion of my sisters' masterpiece. No straight walls, no fancy window lattice. Nonetheless, I do have a chimney pipe and as it happens the can-vas is almost the exact color of gingerbread, and those are the essential ingredients anyway. All the shelter lacks is candy and trimmings, and I can fix that as long as the temperature cooperates with my paints.

I want to start with lollipops, but the colors of my paint aren't, with the exception of yellow, lollipop colors. It takes as long to mix a proper shade as it does to actually paint a fruity orb on the canvas, leaving room for the sticks that I'll add whenever I figure out how to mix brown. As the candy begins to take shape, I envision lollipops lining all around the bottom of the shelter with—a new thought—gumdrops interspersed in between. And that's just the beginning. I'll paint candy canes and holly and giant gingerbread men. *Run run run, as fast as you can,* the childhood story goes, *you can't catch me, I'm the gingerbread man!*

One good chomp, though, and that cocky gingerbread man ended up in the stomach of a very clever fox, and that was the end of that.

I'm so absorbed with my designs that at first I hardly notice the clouds creeping in from the west except that now the paint doesn't gleam so bright on the canvas. I hardly notice the drop in temperature except to wrap my scarf tighter against the wind, and I wouldn't pay it any attention except for the fact that my hands are becoming slightly numb from the cold. Then I notice something I can't ignore. The paint is turning into chunks of ice, just as it did when I painted the juniper, just as it did when the darkness consumed my mind.

The urge to throw the bowl of paint on the ground and stomp on it is almost too strong to resist. Just when I was starting to get a grip . . . just when I was starting to believe I could make it. The desert won't even give me the least little break.

I duck inside the shelter, setting the bowl of paint on the end of the shelf before stooping to add the last few pieces of wood I chopped on Thanksgiving to the stove. As I picture having to walk halfway across the canyon to find more, my heart sinks with dread. Halfway across the canyon is so far. Dragging the wood back is so hard. Nineteen more days is so long, too long, to battle against the darkness.

You are frightened that it will consume you, pulling you into a hole from which there is no return. Truly it may, but only because you allow it. The strange journal entry rises up like a ghost in my mind. I still don't understand where those words came from or what they mean. Reaching for my journal, I flip through the pages until I find the entry.

When one part of you denies its power, another part of you must accept it. The less powerful you believe yourself to be, the more power is given to the darkness. And then you don't believe that the power remains within you, but it does.

I have so often felt powerless—powerless against the darkness, powerless to affect my destiny, powerless to become the woman who looked back at me in the mirror when I searched for my soul as a teenager. All this time I thought I was trying to find her, but maybe I was, after all, trying to outrun her. It's funny how far I ran without even knowing it; from my parents as a teenager, from my marriage, from Alabama. It wasn't relationships that kept me from discovering what I wanted to do with my life, it was fear. If I had dared listen to my heart I would have had no one to blame if I failed. Better not to really try. Better just to say I'm trying while I run run run as fast as I can. I've proved I can run like the wind.

I'm tired of running. I want to prove something new—that I can overcome the darkness, that I can stick it out, that I have the guts to listen to my soul. I want to prove that I'm willing to try to make my dreams come true even if it means failing.

Perhaps thinking of the story of the gingerbread man is reminding me of other childhood tales, because now I remember the *Little Engine that Could,* the train engine that managed to tow an entire line of cars to the top of the steepest hill by telling himself over and over, "I think I can, I think I can." The top of the mountain is within reach if I can just keep chugging. I *have* to make it. Now more than ever, I have to make it.

Painting the shelter was helping. My hands are now warm and if only the paint wasn't frozen—I pick up the bowl and I hardly believe my eyes. The chunks are gone. The paint is smooth liquid. The ice has melted.

In a flash I'm out of the shelter. When I touch the brush to the canvas, the paint adheres as if it never froze, just like normal. After several minutes the paint freezes in the bowl again and I try the same warm-up trick by the wood stove. Sure enough, the paint melts. Sure enough, when I take it outside it still colors the canvas.

I'm overjoyed that the temperature will no longer impede my progress, but I'm concerned about the clouds now rushing in from the west. It still amazes me how quickly the weather can change here. Cold, white mist precedes the clouds, reminding me of the blizzard. My stomach tightens as the wind howls in the cliffs like a warning siren.

I shouldn't have let the firewood supply get so low. It's too late to start off across the canyon. At least the fifty-five-gallon drum is still half full of furniture ends, and with growing unease I stack up a two-day ration by the woodstove. Next I check to make sure there's enough water. The jugs beneath the juniper have remained frozen, and each day I thaw a gallon or so in the frying pan atop the wood stove. It takes a couple of hours to completely melt, so I try not to get caught short. At the moment there's only half a gallon left, so I retrieve two more jugs in case the storm is severe. Fuel, water . . . now food.

I've left the cooler containing the Ziploc baggies of rice and lentils under the juniper with the water jugs, retrieving only daily rations at a time to avoid enticing the mouse with surplus grain. Though the cooler itself is safe against incursion, it's so large that it takes up most of the extra space in the shelter. Nonetheless, I'd rather be crowded than forced to venture outside during a blizzard, so I lug the cooler inside. A count of the remaining baggies proves I brought more than enough food to the desert. Over three-quarters of the Ziploc bags are still full. As often as not I water down the cooked rice and lentils into a soup, and that would have stretched the supply even if my appetite were better. I bet I've lost fifteen pounds.

As the first snowflakes flurry through the air, slamming onto the shelter to make the lollipops glisten with ice like a coating of sugar, I pull the front flap closed from the inside. Whatever Mother Nature has in store for me now, all I can do is hope. I stoke up the wood stove and put on a pot of coffee. At least this time my sleeping bags are dry.

DAY 22, DECEMBER 2, EARLY MORNING

I snip away at the newspaper, snug with my sleeping bag over my legs. I've never attempted to create a gingerbread man pattern three feet tall. Reaching over to add a few sticks of wood to the stove, I pour a little water into the fry pan of simmering juniper needles.

Even its aroma provides companionship in the storm. I'm relieved that though the wind howled all night and snow still swirls in frantic gyrations, this is hardly a blizzard. I've learned what to trust and what to fear. My eyes stray to the wooden crossbeam above my head. I once worried that even a slight breeze would bring it crashing upon my head, but it has held firm through winds far worse than what now blows.

A yawn escapes my lips and I rub my eyes for at least the tenth time. Between the roaring of the wind and the fact that I had no chance to bait the oil can trap—and therefore no reason to hope that the mouse would be detoured from entering the shelter—I didn't sleep well. I buried my head completely under the covers, leaving one tiny opening for the string attached to the fork under the fry pan. When I held the string in my hand I kept accidentally pulling it and tripping the trap, so I tried holding the string in my mouth. I could still jerk it fast if I caught the mouse in the act. Took some getting used to, string in my mouth, but at least I got a few hours of sleep.

The wind begins to settle and the morning passes as I try without success to create a gingerbread man pattern. It has to be *right*. I want my desert Christmas scene to be worthy of Candy Cane Lane.

Candy Cane Lane. I wonder who named it that. It's curious, really, this whole business of naming places. Communities get names. Convention hotels name their meeting rooms and ballrooms. Airports, sporting arenas, shopping malls—they all have names, and so do "special" homes like ranches, houseboats, and retirement property. My parents named their retirement house before it was even built.

Everything except run-of-the-mill regular old family homes

gets a name. Addresses, that's all the regular homes get. But any place can be an address, even if it's Cell Block One. I hear all kinds of talk about how people hate to be referred to as numbers, yet they never get beyond numbering the roof over their own heads. I hold my shelter in higher esteem than to relegate it to "regular house" status. It deserves a name. In honor of the lollipops and gumdrops, and as a fitting abode for even the likes of a gingerbread man, I hereby pronounce it CandyLand.

This is the first time I've ever given my own home a name, if a canvas shelter really counts as a home. It's more than I've got in the outside world, though, and I suspect Thoreau would say that as humble as it is, I could get by for a very long time here or anywhere else. I wish I had a home in the world beyond the desert that could be mine forever. I wouldn't care if it was as primitive as canvas slung over a wooden frame, as long as it was really mine. I'd give it a name and I'd plant a seedling tree just beyond the door and watch it grow year by year, knowing that as its roots reached deeper into the ground, so would my own.

"One spot," Bret Layman said the day he and Dana brought me here. "Long as you got one spot where you feel safe you'll be all right."

I thought he meant a shelter from the desert's dangers, but I don't believe there is a such a shelter. I don't believe there's a spot where I'm truly safe from physical harm, here or in the world beyond. Perhaps Bret meant a different kind of safety: a place where it's safe to be *me*. Here at CandyLand, everything I am is acceptable because there's no one else here to tell me I'm not. My view of the world prevails here as truth, and I'm the only one allowed to dispute it. And when I do decide I'm wrong, I don't ridicule myself. Maybe everyone needs one spot where they can always feel good about who they are. Maybe everyone needs a place where they can invest their hearts and souls and labors, an investment that is as rich as the rewards. I need that.

And I've found that in CandyLand. It's not just the pounding of the nails and the stapling of the canvas. It's not just the efforts at keeping in the warmth and keeping out the mice. It is simultaneously a manifestation of who I am and a vision of who I want to be—and it is the determination to become that woman.

DAY 25, DECEMBER 5, LATE MORNING

Only slight traces of snow remain from the storm, and last night I only woke up twice, just long enough to check that the string was still in my mouth before fading back to sleep. Because most of the snow had cleared, I was finally able to scatter the bread crumbs up the ramp to the oil can, and no pattering of mouse feet disturbed my dreams.

I dare to hope as I circle behind the shelter. The crumbs scattered around the oil can are gone, every last one, but that doesn't surprise me and it isn't necessarily a sign of victory. The crumbs leading all the way up the ramp to the very top, however, are also gone, and that makes my heart beat faster. But there is no corpse in the can.

I can't figure out what I'm doing wrong. My mother didn't have to encourage the mouse at church camp to jump in the bacon grease, but maybe that's the problem. Bacon grease probably appeals more than oil, but *still.* This is getting too frustrating. My mouse probably considers me his best friend in the world, but I am growing weary of playing the cat. In fact, I'm sick of it. If the trap won't work, so be it. I carry the can around to the front of my shelter and place it by the door for later disposal. Right now I've got more pressing things on my mind.

The head, arms and legs of the first gingerbread man begin to take shape as I touch my brush to the shelter, and then the second man emerges and now the third. Fortunately, all my colors mixed together result in a sort of milk-chocolate brown. When the brown is dry, I outline the figures with white, but they still look a little stiff, as if in some way incomplete. And then I realize, *of course,* they have no faces. Wide round blue eyes. Broad red smiles. Circle cheeks. Half-moon noses. Suddenly they come alive.

"Run if you want," I say, painting a blue mitten at the end of each arm, "but don't be surprised if there's mountain lion out there with your name on it." I can't help but be charmed by them.

Maybe that should be enough. As Bret said, this is the desert. Nobody else is going to see CandyLand, so I guess the only point is to please myself. Maybe my purpose in life is to hole up on a deserted island and just be me, creating whatever I want for my own enjoyment. Forget everyone else. But I don't think so. I don't think forgetting everyone else is what the Grand Scheme of Life is meant to be about.

Somehow, in some small way, I want to make a difference in the world. CandyLand is just a shelter in the desert. It's gingerbread boys and hearts on a canvas that will someday rip to shreds. What it *is* probably doesn't count for much in the world beyond the desert at all. But where CandyLand came from does. Its blueprint came from somewhere inside me, some magic place that takes memories and knowledge and hopes and experiences and inspirations and imagination and jumbles them all together and spits out a plan.

I can't pretend that spending forty days in the desert will reveal an exact road map to guide every step of the rest of my life, but I'm learning that I have something to give that no one else in the world could ever give, simply because no one else is me. That is enough. Who I am does matter. In the world beyond the desert there will be other opportunities to create other versions of CandyLand. There will be other opportunities to reach into that magic place within and pull out enough plans for a lifetime and beyond.

They don't have to matter to millions. They don't have to be the cure to all that ails my fellow travelers through life. I just want to do my part, to give whatever being me allows me to give. Through the desert, I'm starting to learn what that is.

Chapter Eighteen

The secret to all fences is posts. If I'd known that before I decided that a fence draped with juniper boughs would give the impression of a tidy little yard around the gingerbread house, I might have given the matter of posts—and post holes—careful consideration. I recall thinking as I entered the desert and counted the fence posts along the road that the feat was impressive, but the post hole digger now joins the mouse trap and the staple gun on my list of the most remarkable of human inventions.

Before setting my heart on the enclosure, I should have concluded that since the ground is frozen it is likely impossible to bury fence posts deep enough that they could then support the considerable weight of juniper boughs. This assumes, of course, that I could first solve the dilemma of what to use for posts, though in comparison to the holes the posts weren't much of a problem. When I ventured across the canyon in search of firewood I found another dead juniper. Its still sturdy limbs fit the bill.

I've tried every implement at my disposal to dig the necessary holes, including my Boy's First Ax, given its ability to double as a plow. The result was a broken ax handle, a possibility that had I foreseen I would have avoided, especially because I made little more than a dent in the frozen ground.

I wish it was as easy as the stone firepit. Anyone can build a firepit because anyone can lift a rock. A child's firepit might be lined with pebbles, whereas a strongman might use boulders, but the size of the stones doesn't essentially alter their functionality. When it comes to chopping wood, however, stronger muscles improve performance, and I've discovered that the same holds true with digging holes for fence posts.

I can't deny that many of the tasks that have for me been a struggle would be a relative piece of cake for most men. From building the shelter to collecting firewood, a male's muscles are simply more dexterous than mine. This observation, of course, did not first arise in the desert. For most of my adult life I've considered such activities as hammering and chopping and moving heavy couches "men's work."

But I wonder where I got the idea that men have certain chores and women have others, because my parents certainly didn't distinguish responsibilities on the basis of sex—probably because they had three daughters and no sons. I mowed the lawn from the time I could push the mower—and our first mower *was* a push mower, not even electric or gas, and the blades were always dull. We had a back yard, a side yard, and a front yard, and the front yard had a steep hill, all of it grassed. Hard work, from which I was never excused because of my gender.

During my teenage years Mom and Dad bought "fixer-uppers,"

houses on the verge of collapse, and restored them with almost no hired help save me and my sisters, a buck an hour. I've roofed and plumbed and scraped and painted. I've pulled up rotting, stinking carpet and laid fresh. I've tiled and glassed and mortared, I've heaved and hoed and hauled. And then I grew up and called it "men's work" and forgot that I once managed quite nicely.

In the past twenty-nine days I've remembered. I am far from helpless. A man might have done it better, but I did build a shelter. A man might have done it faster, but I've managed to gather and—until the broken ax handle—chop firewood. I've kept myself *alive* in the wilderness. True, I didn't have to scavenge for food or water, but I could have died from the cold long before I starved.

I'll always know that I can take care of myself in extreme conditions, and therefore I can take care of myself in less dire circumstances as well. I've always said I can do anything I set my mind to, but now I believe it. The world beyond the desert is filled with reasons I can't make my dreams true, but having stepped away from that world most of the reasons now appear self-imposed. Being removed from society has made it clear that only I can set the limits of my determination. Only I hold the responsibility for my decisions. No one else tells me what's impossible.

And so, if it's the last thing I do, I'll find a way to build this fence.

Because digging post holes in frozen ground without any tools is obviously a futile exertion, I resolve that the first step to success is to look for other alternatives. Fortunately, the example of Christmas trees, or rather, Christmas tree *stands,* comes almost instantly to mind.

Not that Christmas tree stands are easy to operate. As far as I'm concerned they remain unmentioned on the list of mankind's chief achievements. It's very possible that no one will ever build a better mousetrap, but I foresee plenty of room for improvement in the Christmas tree stand department. More than once I've strung up all the lights and garlands and hung all the ornaments and pronounced the tree done—just to discover that although it originally stood straight, the tree now leans noticeably to the left. Usually a minor adjustment of the stand's brackets solves the problem, but one time, just when I thought I got it right, the entire tree fell over, stand and all.

No matter what, stands are tricky, but they're particularly problematic now because I don't have any. Big buckets would be the next best thing—I've known people who put their Christmas tree in a beer barrel filled with dirt and gravel—but I don't have any beer barrels. I don't have any big buckets either. The closest thing, and I'm not sure it's close enough, are the empty water jugs.

By the time I've cut the tops out of the jugs and propped the posts inside and filled all around with gravel, I wish I'd thought of another solution. I see instability in these posts' future. Nonetheless, at the moment they're standing tall and proud.

An hour later the juniper boughs are strung between the posts on the thick wire left over from supporting the stove pipe. The fence looks even better than I'd hoped. As long as no one breathes . . .

DAY 31, DECEMBER 11, LATE AFTERNOON

I'm pleased to see that the warmth has brought back my friend Felipe, or perhaps one of his descendants—hard to be sure with flies.

"Where've you been?" I ask as he zips around my head to land on the slab of stone. The slab is about eighteen by twelve inches and three inches thick and so heavy I can hardly lift it. Felipe seems intently curious.

"It's paint," I say, swishing him away. "Don't get it on your wings or you won't be able to fly. And then you'd die, and then I'd feel guilty." And I would. I'd feel guilty if I killed the mouse, too, but I wish I *could*. Felipe buzzes around my head and takes off again. "See ya," I say, dipping my brush. There. Done. Wait—one more dot—there. The fresh paint gleans in the sun.

Welcome to CandyLand, the stone slab reads, Population: One.

Without much effort, at least in comparison to building the fence or the firepit—the stones I now employ are all smaller than my head—I line both sides of an improvised trail that leads from the top of the wash down into my site up to the "gate." I left a four-foot opening in the juniper bough fence to enter and leave the yard, and it is there that the stone-lined trail ends. At the top the painted stone slab announces to all would-be visitors that they are about to step into another world. Too bad, I think as I survey the scene, that my most regular visitors are mice and flies.

At first the noise of a honking horn is so faint and far away that I'm not startled, only aware, that someone is coming into the canyon. I spot the white truck bouncing over a wash a few hundred yards away. It's an odd time for Bret Layman to make a trip up here. He's never come so close to dark. I'm worried that something is wrong.

It's been *days* since I've seen another human being. I haven't changed my clothes in a month. I must look like a freak.

The truck comes to an abrupt stop a hundred yards from my

site. Bret's steps are brisk and deliberate as I hurry to meet him. He wears a beige coverall suit with an emblem of a duck over the breast pocket. I've never seen him in his work clothes before. He looks official.

"Is everything all right?" I ask. He eyes the ground. "Bret," I say, now thoroughly alarmed, "what's *wrong?*"

He puts his hand on my shoulder and gives it a gentle pat. Shivers run down my spine like an electric shock. It's been so long since I felt someone's touch; so long since I've looked at someone's face. Heat rushes to my cheeks and my voice comes out breathless.

"Is it my son?"

"No," Bret says. "Everyone's fine as far as I know."

I'm even more perplexed. "But—"

"Debi, the BLM knows you're out here."

"What?"

"It's just difficult to keep a secret out here. People talk—even when they don't mean to. Lasso didn't mean no harm."

"*Who?*"

"Lasso—the one who lets the Squirrel Man live on his land. See, about a week ago another one of Lasso's cars broke down, just like they always do. He'd noticed your car parked at the wildlife refuge for nearly a month, and he thought it might be for sale. I told him no, it wasn't—it belonged to you. Squirrel Man had already mentioned meeting you, of course, so Lasso knew who you were and what you were up to.

"So Lasso was at the post office inquiring if anybody in town might be selling a car, and as people 'round here do, he got to talking and mentioned to the postmaster that he'd tried to buy the car right out from underneath that little gal who's spending forty days in the wilderness.

"Bill—that's the postmaster—he never would have said noth-ing about it. But it so happened that some freelance writer from Chicago stopped in to inquire about faxing her article on the Pony Express trail—that's why she was in Calleo, to write an article—and she overheard Lasso tell Bill about your retreat.

"Lasso said he'd never seen two eyes shine so bright. She marched right up to him and practically begged him to take her to where you are. Said it'd make a fabulous article for her magazine. She even promised she'd put Lasso's name in it, but she didn't know that that's about the last thing in the world Lasso wants. Lasso told her he was sorry but he couldn't help her because he didn't know where exactly you were staying, only that you were somewhere on BLM land."

"Oh God," I say.

"She stopped by the wildlife refuge and saw your car. I was out in the marshes at the time, but the other rangers knew enough to keep their mouths closed. She said she didn't have time to wait. I figured we'd heard the last of her, but we hadn't. When she got back to Chicago she called the BLM and asked if they knew your whereabouts. Of course they didn't, and apparently they read her the riot act about how it's illegal and dangerous and that no woman by herself ought to be out in the desert with nobody knowing where she is. The writer told them that *somebody* must know where you are because your car is parked at the wildlife refuge, and un-less you hiked into the wilderness then somebody took you."

"And that somebody is you," I say.

"The BLM agent for our region called yesterday," Bret nods. "I happened to be out in the marshes. Today I told the office that if he calls again, tell him I'm not in. They covered for me this time but I'm not sure how long this can go on."

My mind races to count the days. Eight more after today.

"I just don't know how stirred up he is," Bret says. "There's nothing to prevent him from sending out the search team."

"The desert's a big place," I say.

"Thing is, I work for the government too. All this BLM guy has to do is call my boss and I'm out of a job. If you were to get hurt and I hadn't come clean, it'd be my tail they'd come after. You can bet they'd come after it good."

"But they can't push me out now," I say. "I can take *care* of myself, Bret, I've proved that I can."

"Like the Squirrel Man said, it's not like they're motivated entirely by your well-being. You're breaking their rules. If you get away with it, what's to prevent others from doing the same thing? People have been hurt—even killed—on public lands, and the government's gotten sued."

"I'm so sorry," I say. "I never thought it would come to this."

"I'll try to head him off," Bret says, "but I can't make any promises." His eyes look past me and I follow his gaze to my painted gingerbread house. "You did all that?"

"I guess you could call it my one spot," I say.

"Dana would go crazy over it," Bret says. "Mind if I take a closer look?"

As Bret circles the shelter, it sinks in even deeper how much this place has come to mean to me. It isn't *right* that the BLM could make me leave. This is my world—the BLM knows nothing about it. They don't know about the witch who turned the giant into stone. To them Pisa Rock is just a rock. They haven't followed the rivulets after a rain to see where they disappear. They don't know about the one juniper that stands taller and prouder than all the others. They don't know about Felipe or how Candy-Land got its name.

I don't claim permanent possession. I don't mean to deny the BLM its authority. But I can't leave. All I ask is to fulfill my forty days, and then this canyon's stories will once again whisper in the wind. If I have to I will run run run away from the BLM, and if I can't run fast enough I'll find a way to dig a hole in the frozen ground and hide. I'll do whatever I have to do.

Bret circles back, shaking his head. "I just can't get over what you've done. Talk about Christmas. Dana's been after me to hang lights on our roof. The other rangers started the day after Thanksgiving and she says we ought to do our share. I say, what's the point? Nobody's going to see them way out here in the middle of nowhere."

"It's nicer when people can appreciate it," I say.

"Yeah," Bret says, "but that's part of life in the desert. You know, a month ago I wouldn't have bet that you'd last three days. When that blizzard hit and Dana and I couldn't get up here, I thought for sure we'd find you either dead or nuts. But now— look what you've done."

"I almost walked out of here two weeks ago."

"But you didn't. Hey, great sign. Population: One."

"For now, anyway," I say, thinking that if the BLM pulls me out, it'll be Population: Zero. Even the Little Engine That Could couldn't have if they'd pulled the tracks out from under him.

Chapter Nineteen

When the rustling begins outside the shelter I hold perfectly still. I've been awake for hours worrying about the BLM, praying for dawn, so eluded by sleep that I long ago lit the candle on the bedside table so I wouldn't have to just lay in the dark. Now I'm glad I couldn't sleep. The moment has finally come for me to finish off Little Sport. Thanks to the candlelight I'll be able to see the little monster when he dares to invade. He'll wish he'd gone for the oil when he had a chance.

The rustling stops and I hold my breath, imagining his beady eyes and pointy nose poking through some crack I've somehow overlooked. His whiskers shiver as he tries to make up his mind. *To dart or not to dart, that is the question.*

The rustling comes again, now louder and more urgent. But no closer. My ears are so attuned to the night that I'm sure of that. He's still outside. I'm amazed a mouse could make so much noise.

It sounds more like scratching, really, like fingernails running up and down a tin can. I raise my head, trying to pinpoint the direction. Just outside the shelter, somewhere between here and the juniper where the water jugs are stored. The scratching is a bit unnerving. I'm beginning to wish the mouse would just go away. Leave the trapping for another day, that's what I wish.

"Shoo," I call out in what I hope is a don't-mess-with-me voice. "Go on, now. Shoo."

The scratchy rustle makes a sudden startled sound and then it's quiet. Almost too quiet. Until now I was positive the noise was the mouse, but doubt is a strange thing, working its way into one's mind like an unpredictable tide. It had to have been the mouse, except I've never heard a mouse make that much commotion.

Minutes later another rustle, another scratching, and my stomach goes hollow.

In thirty-two nights I've heard a myriad of desert sounds. Twigs breaking, pebbles falling, wind whispering. The roar of the jets' engines and the rumble of Bret's Toyota. Phantom phones and radios, music in the fire. The hammer connecting to iron nails, the stapler penetrating a wooden frame. The hiss and sputter of the propane burner, the hesitant *whoosh* as the lantern flares to white light. The crunch of my own footsteps in the snow and the plop of raindrops on the canvas. The growls of my stomach, the groans of a frozen water jug melting on the wood stove, the splashing when I washed my hair. The distinct pitter-patter of the mouse's tiny paws across my shelter floor—and this is not that sound or any other that I've heard before.

Even after all this time I'm afraid of the sound that might come right before the canvas rips open and a mountain lion leaps into the shelter to sink his teeth into my throat. I'm still afraid of the sound that means the Midnight Stalker lurks in the canyon awaiting the perfect moment to attack. And now, when the rustling continues louder and even more insistent, I can't stop my mind from jumping to the most horrific conclusions. I can't make my heartbeat slow down. I can't keep the desperation from taking control.

I reach under my pillow for the hatchet. If only the candle wasn't lit—darkness is my best defense. But if I blow it out now, whatever's out there will know I've heard it. But it already knows. Yelling "shoo" was probably a dead giveaway. The wick glows for several long seconds after my breath extinguishes the flame.

Whether it's man or beast, it isn't afraid of me, that much is certain. It rattles just beyond the shelter as if it's trying to bait me into coming out. I won't fall into that trap. If it wants me, it'll have to come get me. The lion will have to choose his target. The madman will have to choose where to slash his knife. If they miss me on the first try, the advantage becomes mine.

Every muscle in my body tenses and I slide to my knees and silently raise the hatchet, gripping the handle hard with both hands, harder when the scratching comes again. I now realize with lethal certainty that I will fight to the death. I'd rather face a man than a mountain lion, but one skull is as vulnerable as the other. The rustling stops, and then it starts again. I know its intent—to madden me, confuse me, push me over the edge, but I won't be pushed. A lion's instincts are sharp but my wits are sharper. A madman may be the more ruthless, but I am the more sane. Whatever it is won't take me without a battle.

At first the change is so slight that it's hardly perceptible. At first I'm not even sure. Perhaps my eyes are simply becoming accustomed to the darkness, but they should have been accustomed long before now. Until now, however, the shelter was so dark that I couldn't discern even the outlines of the painted figures on the canvas, but in the last few minutes the gingerbread men seem to have emerged from the shadows.

My knees ache from sitting in one position too long. My arms are exhausted from holding the hatchet in assault mode. As the shapes on the walls grow increasingly clear, a new form of doubt enters my mind. If either mountain lion or madman wanted me dead, surely I would have known it hours ago. With agonizing quiet I finally shift off my knees and scoot to the door. I push it open just an inch and press my eye to the crack. Slowly, I push the flap open.

The minutes seem suspended in time, dangling on a held breath as I dare to force my head through the flap. I wince, half expecting a lion to pounce from atop my shelter and knock me into instant blackness. Gripping the hatchet tight, I push my shoulders through the flap, my eyes darting frantically to take in my entire surroundings at once, knowing too well that I'm vulnerable to the rear. I come to my feet and swing around, my knees nearly buckling to be relieved of their strain.

Best I could tell, the sounds came from somewhere near the juniper. Sure that I now feel the eyes of some creature following my every move, I examine the frozen water jugs. Each is upright. None appear to have been moved. I press my face close to the ground covered with brittle brown juniper needles that crackle under my weight. But that isn't the sound I heard in the night.

As the mystery deepens, so does my concern. Walking all around my site I find nothing amiss, not even the juniper bough fence. The posts would have tipped over at the slightest provocation.

Each day the wind blows over at least one. Each day I repair the damage, but whatever rustled in the night made no impact on the fence.

Drenched in relief at not being jumped by a madman, the longer my inspection continues without providing clues, the more I begin to question the validity of the fear that kept me propped up all night with a hatchet in my hand; in fact, the more I begin to feel a bit foolish. That's the trouble with fear. It takes one tiny grain of truth and exaggerates it a thousand times so that it actually contradicts common sense. Common sense tells me that a scratching sound in the middle of the night is unusual—*fear* says the sound must be a madman or a lion.

I knew the desert hadn't cured me of all fear but I thought I'd at least learned to tell when there's actually something to be afraid of. Having scrutinized every square inch of my site without finding so much as a track in the snow, I'm stumped—a condition that seems best accompanied by a cup of coffee. I open the shelter flap and begin to crawl inside when my foot kicks the can full of oil that I intended to dispose after it failed to attract the mouse. Indeed, the problem of disposal may now have solved itself, and I turn around to see if my kick managed to knock over the can.

A glance is all it takes to be assured that the can remains upright, but in that same glance a particle of . . . something . . . on the surface catches my eye. My heart skips a beat and I lean a little closer. It's a tiny black body with limp wings. A fly.

"Oh, Felipe," I moan. "Oh, Felipe." My one and only desert friend. Gone. It's not fair. I wouldn't have hurt him, not for the world.

I owe him the best burial I can manage in the frozen ground. Retrieving a spoon from the shelter, I scrape a small area under a juniper clear of needles and return to the oil can for the body. I skim the surface of the oil. Felipe lands on the spoon but slides off and disappears under the cloudy surface. I dip deeper, stirring the ooze until something dark and—at first it looks small—rises to the surface. But in the next instant I realize the dark spot is the tip of an iceberg, a mass that grows bigger before my eyes.

Nothing could brace me for what I see. It's not just one. There is no mistaking the shape—the shapes. Oil drips from the spoon as I pull up the first and slide the lifeless body to the ground. I dip the spoon again, and then again, and three times more. Six now lay in a row of mass execution. Six mice. They must have jumped in. No fry-bread bait, no ramp. They simply jumped.

Horror pumps through my veins as I realize exactly what I heard in the night—and why it came and went. Each time I heard a rustling, another mouse jumped into the oil; each scraping was a desperate attempt to climb out of the can. I picture their tiny claws scraping and slipping against the tin, each silence meaning a moment of death. Six mice, dead at my hand.

I raise from my knees, brushing juniper needles from my pants. Nature being nature, chances are good the bodies won't last long before they end up in a stomach of a very clever fox—or badger or skunk or whatever else happens to sniff them out. I feel bad that I couldn't offer the mice a more peaceful eternity. And yet, with six nights remaining of my retreat I'll leave the oil can outside my shelter door and hope a dozen more meet the same fate if it keeps them out of my bed.

Thoreau said that "the very simplicity and nakedness of man's life in the primitive ages imply this advantage at least, that they left him but a sojourner in Nature." I suspect that there's really no such thing as being only a sojourner, an innocent bystander just passing through. Even primitive man must have taken out a few mice. Maybe six mice don't really matter in the whole scheme of things, but I wonder what the desert's breaking point will be. I wonder what the earth's breaking point will be, when humans have mined one lump of coal too many, pumped one drop of oil too much, chopped down the one tree that made the difference between enough oxygen and not.

I can't deny that my presence has affected this canyon. Not, I suspect, permanently. The mouse population will recover. By next winter there will be dead juniper limbs aplenty beneath the living trees, just as there were before I came and burned the current supply. But it makes me sad to realize how hard it is to find a place where one can legally spend forty days and nights in the desert, or any other wilderness. A hundred years ago a person had to make an effort to get *out* of the wilds. Now it's an effort to get in. If my son ever decides to retreat to the wilderness, I wonder whether there will be any wilderness left.

Day 34, December 14, early afternoon

Despite concern that every hour may be my last before the BLM finds me, I continue to make progress at CandyLand. Everything fits together to create a Christmas wonderland—except the tree. I'm now quite sure that the Christmas tree tradition did *not* originate in the desert. No one would ever think to chop down a scraggly juniper and stick it in their living room. I had to walk halfway across the canyon to find an alternative, a young cedar, five feet tall. At least it's the right shape, but it still has no decorations. Even the juniper berries that I strung into a longer version of my party necklace don't really look like garlands. They look like part of the tree.

My only hope is the box of craft supplies. Five little pots of paint, each less than a quarter full. Scissors. Wire. Staples. Staple gun. Paintbrush. Hunk of clay, and that's what I'm after.

The clay is stiff in my fingers as I break off a small lump and roll it between my palms. The ball begins to crumble. I sprinkle a few drops of water on my hands, and now the clay becomes smooth and hard. It takes practice to know when clay has reached the proper consistency. Not moist enough, it crumbles. Too moist, clay is mud.

I squash the ball flat in my hands, pat it into a circle about two inches wide and a third of an inch thick, and puncture a hole through the clay with a ball point pen. When it's fired and painted, a piece of string tied through the hole, it might look something like a Christmas tree ornament.

As I break off another chunk of clay, my hands turn the color of brick. From a chunk comes a ball, the ball presses flat, the clay takes the shape my hands decide. For thirty-four days I have been clay in the desert's hands, pulled this way, stretched that way. It's hard to imagine that I will soon wake up in a world where different forces pull me this way and that. I've become so accustomed to the cliffs and the sage and the junipers that I don't know how my eyes will cope with skyscrapers and sprawling shopping malls and cement parking lots. I've become so accustomed to the quiet that I wonder how my ears will respond to cars honking, radios blasting, phones ringing off the hook.

It'll be a long time before I crave rice and chickpea lentils. I won't miss collecting firewood, but I will miss the campfires. I will miss the desert's dramatic simplicity. I will miss its system of justice. I will miss the peace.

If I had to choose between spending the rest of my life entirely within the confines of a city or entirely in the wilderness, I would choose the wilderness. I can't imagine a life in which the only place to encounter Nature is a zoo. If I couldn't live where Nature is free, I would feel as if I were the one in the cage. My regret over the mice and concern for the shrinking wilderness has become a determination: wherever my *home* may turn out to be, whatever niche of this planet I find to call mine forever, it can't be where humans have replaced what once was with their own interpretation of how the world should look. I don't want fire and stones and sunsets to become only distant memories, the only remnants of a life I left in the desert.

DAY 37, DECEMBER 17, MORNING

Ancient firing techniques required that clay be fully dried in the sun before its exposure to fire, but that could take more time than I have because the temperature rarely breaks freezing. I light a small fire and arrange the clay pieces as close to the flames as I dare. The heat, I hope, will speed up the process, but if the ornaments get too hot too fast they could explode.

When the ornaments have turned gray, I'm still not certain whether they've been colored by ash or are actually dry, but I add a couple of logs to the fire and edge the ornaments closer to the flames. I know I'm rushing it, but I don't have time. Seventy-two hours left, but maybe only one. It all depends on whether Bret has been able to head off the BLM.

A sudden *pop* in the firepit sends dirt and clay shrapnel flying, followed by a second pop. Fragments blow out of the ash and shards scatter at my feet, and now it sounds like popcorn in the fire. I grab the shovel and scoop ornaments out of the flames, exploding faster than I can rescue them.

The morning is spent painting the survivors. Yellow and blue and green circles, striped candy canes, red hearts. When the first coat dries, I paint white snowflakes on some, holly and evergreen trees on others. I *am* clay. For thirty-seven days I have faced the same test of fire and I did not explode.

One by one I hang the ornaments on the tree, the largest on the stronger lowest branches, the smaller ornaments up higher. And with that the tree is done.

It's all done. CandyLand is done.

I walk through the juniper bough gate and up the stone-lined path to the top of the wash. For a long moment I stare out across the valley floor at white sand dotted with sage. Today the mountains in the west seem to envelope the desert in a protective embrace, holding the world beyond at bay. Turning back toward my site I draw in a sudden breath. There are times the eyes give their beholder the wondrous gift of seeing something familiar as if for the first time, and for a moment I feel as though I am six years old, holding my grandfather's hand as a cat and mouse chase each other around the bed where Ma and Pa snore on unaware.

My grandfather taught me the meaning of Christmas. My vision of CandyLand came to me through him. I've been so angry with him for not understanding my choices, so crushed that he shut me out of his life. But maybe it was I who shut him out. Each time I set the bowl of frozen paint to melt by the wood stove, my own heart melted a little more. I ache to tell my grandfather that he is CandyLand's inspiration, that despite the times he hasn't been proud of me, we can both be proud of this. I ache to be able to say *I made it, Grandpa, I made it all forty days.*

The morning after the blizzard, when I climbed the slope and looked down at my battered tent, I believed I'd been given the gift of a second chance. And now I feel as if I am once again climbing that slope, each day reaching higher and higher, looking down at the person who survived the blizzard and stayed. I did not explode in the desert's fire, and so I have been transformed. I have been made strong, strong enough to need my grandfather's love more than I need to be right. When I leave this place I will offer my hand to him in peace.

DAY 38, DECEMBER 18, LATE AFTERNOON.

A vague sense of unease stirs through my body as if to remind me of something I'd forgotten. I've become so accustomed to correlating my activities to the sun's position that I don't even consciously decide it's time to begin the evening's chores. I simply feel the unease as the shadows lengthen and the light changes angle.

Intent upon heating leftover rice and lentil soup for my dinner, I pause under the juniper outside my shelter to retrieve a gallon of water to melt for dishes. There are only three gallons left. I'll barely have enough to make it two more days. On the first day of my retreat when I stacked the jugs under the tree, I didn't know if I'd last long enough to use up six gallons, much less all sixty-four. I've never before marked time in units of water jugs.

When I was a child, my great-grandmother made an advent

calendar that each year my mother hung in a place of honor next to the fish tank in our living room hallway. The calendar was a three-foot felt Christmas tree on a burlap background, and though my great-grandmother had glued jewels and lace garlands onto the tree, she had also sewn twenty-five hooks—the type from hooks and eyes—among the branches. She had then collected miniature ornaments, which she wrapped individually in white tissue.

Each year, starting on December 1 and continuing until Christmas day, my sisters and I took turns reaching into a box to choose a single tissue-wrapped packet. We crowded around as that morning's selector peeled back the paper to reveal the delicate ornament—a toy soldier or a wreath, bells or tiny packages or an angel. The girl whose turn it was got to choose where to hang the ornament on the tree. Every morning the tree grew one ornament fuller. Every ornament brought Christmas one day closer.

My great-grandmother had provided a total of fifty or so ornaments, and because only twenty-five went on the tree any given year, the finished product never looked quite the same as it did the year before. My sisters and I never tired of the tradition, as evidenced by the annual argument over who would make the first selection.

The important thing, I think, was that because we weren't allowed to wait until Christmas Eve and then pull twenty-four ornaments out of the box and decorate the tree all at once, each of the twenty-three days before then *mattered*. Christmas wasn't just the day itself, it was also the days leading up to it. The goal of seeing the tree fully decorated was always foremost in our minds, but each day we appreciated the single ornament that brought the final goal closer.

As an adult I'm not sure I've appreciated time in the same

way. I don't recall ever turning to a new page on the calendar and thinking *Here come the next thirty days of my life. Each day will matter, each day will contribute to the whole, and at the end of this month I'll look back and see all I've accomplished.*

When I came to the desert, however, I knew I would look back. I hoped these forty days would change my life—and they have, but so did every other forty days before that. The difference was that I didn't notice. I wasn't focused on trying to make something happen. Not that I want to radically alter my direction every forty days, but that's the point. The past forty days have helped me define a course that I believe I can pursue the rest of my life. I will leave here with the three-foot-tall felt Christmas tree on burlap, jeweled and laced—but with empty hooks scattered among the branches.

With the last of the sunlight becoming the day's memory, I hurry to complete my chores. The floor still needs sweeping with the dishtowel but I can hardly make out the floor in the dimness of dusk. The lantern would do the trick, but I take the label warnings of asphyxiation seriously. Even when I've used the propane stove I've always opened the shelter flap for circulation, and I'm not crazy about having the flap open this close to dark. Prime mouse time. Well, just this once.

I place the lantern atop my bedside table, pump the pressure, turn the metal lever that supposedly cleans out the gas chamber and finally hold a match to the mantels. The resulting beam is truly striking in comparison to the usual candlelight—another leap up the ladder of progress. It's even brighter than daylight, which shouldn't surprise me since sunlight must filter through the canvas. The lantern's light is so bright, bouncing and reflecting off the canvas, that the objects painted on the outside are invisible from within, just as the effect of stained glass is lost to those inside the church when it's dark outside and totally bright within.

Thanks to the light, however, this evening's sweeping job is by far more effective than usual, and I scoop up a small pile of dust in the towel. It's silly, really. I could just lean out the door and shake the towel clean, but I can't help but think that then I'd track that very same dust right back in. One chance is all I'm willing to give dust before I burn it, so I take the towel out to the firepit and shake it clean.

Then I turn around to head back to the shelter, but what I see stops me short.

After all those Christmas Eve services, I should have remembered. When it's dark outside and bright inside, the stained glass is stunning. My shelter is *glowing*. Until this moment I thought that given my inability to string Christmas lights from cliff to cliff, CandyLand could never rival the Candy Cane Lane of my childhood, but I have never in my life seen anything quite like this. The gingerbread boys, the lollipops, the candy canes and gumdrops and hearts and holly, every figure is aglow, casting the snow all around in a peach halo.

All I can do is stare as the emotions I've felt during these thirty-eight days seem to mix and swirl inside me like the colors of the sunset. I feel the panic of watching Bret's Toyota drive out of sight for the first time, but I also feel the tenderness of having come to know this place so well. I feel the vulnerability of the desert peeling away the layers of my defenses, and I feel it bringing forth my strengths. I feel the discouragement and the hope. This is the sunset on my day in the desert, and like that moment before the sun slips below the horizon, I feel the pride of reaching a goal and the subtle sorrow of moving on.

Chapter Twenty

The garlands are first to go. I unravel each bough and release the posts from the water jugs. The fire blazes as I toss the limbs atop it and dark smoke billows high in the air. My gingerbread house looks like a fort without defense in the absence of its tidy border, but I knew all along it was borrowed. Now I must return it.

The Christmas tree is next. I tuck each ornament between folds of newspaper, carefully, tenderly, for they are my sole creations of CandyLand that will leave the desert. Someday, I will give them to my son. I hope whenever he looks at them he will always remember that who he is matters. I hope that he'll look into the mirror and dream of the life he wants to live. I hope he'll someday ask himself what he'd do if he was the last person on earth. I hope he'll have the courage to find his own one spot.

I pick up a stone from the rim of the firepit, the pit that began as bare ground and became the stone cathedral that rang with the flame's music. The stone is bigger than my head and reminds me of a miniature half-moon. One side is smooth and black from smoke. The other side is round and crated. I wonder how long it had been just where it was when I found it. I wonder if its life began deep in the bowels of the planet to become part of the cliffs as the earth's crust stretched, or whether it ever lay buried beneath a prehistoric saline sea.

I place the stone next to the bundle of ornaments. This ancient building block will accompany me into the future.

The last task is to clean off the shelf. Toiletries, candles, Tony's Little League photo, and finally the Cherokee mask. Its wide eyes seem to look all the way to my heart.

"I hope," Jerry said when he placed the mask in my hands, "that when you find your answers you will also find ours."

I have found all the answers that I can find alone. Only by returning to the world beyond the desert will I discover whether I found enough answers for two.

It's nearing dark before I've completed packing. A mound of supplies now awaits Bret's truck. Sixty-three plastic jugs are stowed in five plastic garbage bags. In one afternoon I've demolished almost everything that took forty days to create. Only the shelter survives, but in its emptiness it is ghostly, as if my absence is already realized. I can't bring myself to tear it down. Over time the desert will do the job itself.

I strike a match under a wad of newspapers piled high with dead sage and as much firewood as I could find. The sage smolders reluctantly as if it understands that the sooner it bursts to life, the sooner its end will come.

I settle into the director's chair and tuck Dana's parka close around me as I have done so many times, and now this is the last.

I wouldn't have made it without the jacket. I wouldn't have made it without the wood stove or the furniture ends or the staples or the little nails. I wouldn't have made it through if I had truly been left here alone. Maybe it's "cheating" to count on others in the pursuit of our dreams, but I don't think so. I think it's cheating to think that any of us are islands unto ourselves. I think it's cheating to be blind to the kindness and wisdom of others, crediting only ourselves with our achievements.

As the flames leap higher and higher, a deviant spark shoots fifteen feet into the air and extinguishes into nothing with a soft sigh. It's so quiet that my heartbeat makes an audible *pabump, pabump.* And then I hear the long, low note, floating from the coals. The first is followed by another as if played by a pipe organ in a church. Five more notes follow and then the melody repeats over.

I tip my head back just as a shooting star blazes across the heavens, the first and only one I've seen in all the nights I've watched the desert sky. A shiver runs down my spine as I wonder where I'll be the next time I see one. I wonder if I will ever again be where it is quiet enough to hear the music in the fire.

DAY 40, DECEMBER 20, MORNING

Bret Layman arrives shortly after sunrise. Together we load the remainder of my supplies into his truck.

"I'm glad to be leaving this way," I say, "instead of at the BLM's insistence."

"Guess the joke was on all of us," Bret says, lifting the cooler. "Finally occurred to me to check a BLM map. Only half the canyon is under their jurisdiction and you're not on that half. The rest is semi-allocated to the school system, but I don't think anybody really knows who it belongs to."

"After all that," I say, shaking my head.

He chuckles. "Is this the last of your stuff?"

"I'll double-check." I duck into the shelter and the fragrance of juniper needles lingers in the air. There, where my coffee brewed; there, where I cooked my rice and lentils. There, where I wrote in my journal; there, where I poured cupful after cupful of water over my head and became, for one short night, the most sensuous creature on earth. There, where the mouse slipped in; there, where the ghosts of my relatives floated in my dreams. There, where I trimmed a gingerbread-boy pattern; there, where I slept with my head buried and a string in my mouth. No longer does my bedding cover the floor. No longer are my toiletries and mementos pleasantly cluttered on the shelf. There, only memories remain.

I push through the front flap, banging my shin as I follow. Bret offers his hands. "You all right?"

"Happens all the time," I say, rubbing my leg. "I never quite got the doorway fixed right."

"You did a good job with the rest of it," Bret says.

"It kept me warm and dry," I say, and our eyes meet. We both know that the shelter was more than that. "I guess the Squirrel Man will be after the canvas now. At least it won't rot."

"Wouldn't worry too much," Bret says. "He was probably more interested before you painted lollipops and candy canes all over it."

"Yeah," I say. "I can hear him now. *Waste of a fine piece of fabric.*" I pull the flap closed and recall all the nights that I pulled it as snug as I could before crawling into my sleeping bags. "I never closed it from the outside. There's no way to secure it." My voice raises a notch. "Bret, I can't just leave without closing the door behind me."

"Maybe tack a nail," Bret suggests.

I look into the eyes of this gentle man, knowing our paths may never cross again. If I've learned something about self-reliance in these past forty days, I've also learned that I never want to be the last person on earth. Without Bret, I wouldn't have found this canyon. Without Bret, I might not have emerged alive. Perhaps unknowingly, he played a role not only in my life but in the lives of all those I know and love.

Minutes later the job is done. The flap is sealed, the door is closed.

"You ready?" Bret asks.

"One last thing." I walk to the top of the wash where the painted slab is propped against a boulder. Welcome to CandyLand. Population: One. I turn the slab face down. Population: Zero.

I slide in the Toyota beside Bret.

"Ready."

Epilogue

DAY 1,829, 5:35 P.M.

It's the wrong time of year for fireflies, but the sparks that shoot ten feet from the blazing fire into the December sky remind me that warmer days will within a few months prompt the flashing bugs' return to the Alabama woods. I hold my hands close to the fire and rub them together. The exposure to the night's chill is self-imposed. A few steps away a doorway framed with blinking Christmas lights leads inside the cabin where it is cozy and warm.

The firepit, in the center of a brick patio, is composed of local stones—except one. Cratered on one side, smooth on the other, this rock once belonged to the firepit in the desert. When I first brought it here, five years ago now, it lay on bare ground raked clear of debris. The patio came two years after I emerged from the desert. In the spring, flower beds lush with roses and dahlias and cannas and impatiens stretch from the patio to the edge of the woods; the flower beds took a few years of nurturing before they matured. Everything took time.

Some things happened faster than others. I left the desert four days before Christmas and drove to my grandparents' home in California to reunite with my family. Grandpa basically ignored me from the moment I arrived, but then again he basically ignored everyone. He slept practically all the time, and when he was awake he didn't seem certain where he was. He snored while my father read *A Christmas Carol,* even during Dad's rendition of Scrooge's nephew's laughter.

And then on Christmas Eve my grandfather suddenly snapped out of it. He got out of bed, sat up in his easy chair and ate a hearty dinner. Grandma said she hadn't seen him so alert in months. I caught him alone while everyone else was doing the dishes. I knelt by his side and let the words spill out, everything that I had been aching to tell him.

"Maybe we can't see eye to eye on everything, Grandpa," I finished, laying my head on his knee, "but that doesn't mean we don't love each other."

He didn't answer for so long that I thought he'd fallen asleep without having heard a word I said, but then I felt his hand stroke my head. "I'm proud of you," he said. Those simple words, that short moment, healed the distance between us. My grandfather died eight months later.

He never got to see our home. Jerry and I named it "Tanager" in honor of the bright red birds that spend their summers in our forest. Each May the tanagers land in the oaks behind the cottage to announce their return from the Mayan rain forests of Central America. In their annual journey across the Gulf of Mexico, nearly eighty percent perish. Each time the survivors find their way back to Tanager I'm reminded that I too could have lost my way in my own journey home.

I brought my "one spot" with me. Just as copper and zinc combine to produce brass, so too have Jerry and I created a home together that neither of us could have created alone. Along with the patio, firepit, flower beds and ponds, the cabin itself no longer bears resemblance to a tree house except for the fact that it's tall and narrow; on one side the additional room, our bedroom, rises to meet the original structure with a glass-paned slanting ceiling that reaches twenty feet at its highest. The original tree house with Tony's loft rises fifteen feet above that.

Tony is now fourteen, slender and as tall as I, with muscles just beginning to show the promise of manhood. He flies to Alabama each Christmas and Easter and for his summer breaks. In the winter he still sleeps in the loft, though during the summer he prefers a sleeping bag on the deck, a deck he helped build. His favorite time is at dusk, when he crumbles bread at the entrance to one of the trails I raked back into the woods. Within minutes the first of the raccoons arrives for the daily feast, soon followed by possums and three foxes. Tony is growing up to know the value of fire, stones and sunsets.

Our forest acreage adjoins thousands more that have so far gone untouched by the lumberjacks and is filled with wild turkeys, deer, honeybees, bats, squirrels and a myriad of birds and reptiles whose natural habitats are rapidly shrinking. It is here that my experience in the desert has found its most profound relationship to my life in the outside world. We are taking steps to protect our land into perpetuity that it may always remain a natural habitat. We've begun drawing blueprints for a new and larger home, which when finished will allow the tree house-cabin to become a guest house. In time we hope to add other cottages for visiting writers and artists and other groups interested in wildlife and ecology. If I have anything to say about it, there will be at least one wilderness area forever safe from harm.

Home means more to me than ever because I now spend the spring in Italy and the fall in New England working as a tour director, escorting groups on vacation and providing educational commentary on the region and sites visited. It took time to find a job that could contribute to my goals rather than detract from them, but I've discovered that there's more than one way to sail the seven seas.

I think my grandfather would have approved.

Grandma stayed in the house for a few years after he died and then she moved to a retirement community. She invited all the family to take what they wanted from the house because she wouldn't have room in her new apartment. I was the last to go through Grandpa's bookshelves before Grandma had scheduled an estate seller to dispose of everything left. As I picked among the books, some rare first editions, others complete sets of unabridged works, I pulled out one particularly thick and dusty volume, so old that the title had worn off its leather cover. I noticed a bulge where someone had placed a packet of something among the pages, and then it slipped free.

The contents, stacked sheets of paper folded in half, were contained in a sandwich bag. My lips began to tremble as I realized what I'd found.

Marley was dead; to begin with. There is no doubt whatever about that.

The opening lines of *A Christmas Carol*. The entire book was contained in the loose-leaf pages. But this was not the bound copy Grandpa pulled from his shelf every Christmas Eve to read aloud.

There was no cover at all, only sheets, and on the first page, in Grandpa's handwriting, was scrawled: *This is the copy sent overseas by my wife, 7 and 8 pages at a time, for me to read to my fellow soldiers during a time of war. May this copy never be needed again.*

I don't know how such things happen, but I've always thought that maybe Grandpa wanted me to be the one to find that packet. As I held those pages I could almost hear him say, "It wasn't too late for Scrooge, and it wasn't too late for us." Because of forty days and forty nights in the desert, it wasn't.

May it never be too late for any of us. May we each always feel the "apoplectic opulence" within our hearts. May we all look into our own eyes and see the life our soul offers. Sometimes, after all, it is only a matter of what we're willing to do to find it.

Acknowledgments

The publication of this book is a dream come true, but like most worthwhile endeavors, it has also been a mighty challenge. On more days than I care to count, Tony entertained himself while I labored at the computer over draft after draft of the manuscript. Thanks, Tony, for your tolerance, and thanks for believing in your mother. I love you with all my heart.

Without others who believed, this dream would not have come to fruition. Thank you to Linda Konner, my agent, and a giant thank you to Faith Conlon, my editor, and to everyone else at Seal Press. Faith, you are dynamite. To Randy Durband at Tauck Tours, thanks for taking a chance on the gal in the hat. To Kendra Beardslee St. John, also at Tauck Tours, thanks for being considerate of my circumstances and for the opportunity to work at a fulfilling occupation that has also allowed time to pursue my other goals. You're terrific.

Thanks to Kathy T. De Master, a special friend who was the first person in whom I confided my desert plan. Instead of telling me I was crazy, she encouraged me to follow my heart. Two other women have extended that kindness to me almost my entire life. To Sue Wiseman and Phyllis, my gratitude for your friendship and love. Thank you so very, very much.

In addition to my mother, who was my Girl Scout leader throughout elementary school, I want to thank Jean Buxton and Lisa Pederson for the many years that they devoted their time, talents, tender care and exceptional patience to my teenage Girl Scouting experience. Please, everyone, when the "Girls in Green" come around to your door, share a little of your own green and buy those cookies.

I feel incredibly lucky that of all the people in the world I could have been raised by and with, I got a handful of the best. To Lois and George Blanks, my mom and dad, thanks for giving me the rare gift of an interesting childhood. It set a high standard for the rest of my life, and I will be forever in awe of you. To my sisters, Dorothy and Caroline, thank you for the shining examples of the type of woman I want to be. I'm so proud of you both. To Gina, if I had ever had my own daughter I would have wanted her to be you. To Uncle Bert, thanks for the ballet lessons and a little girl's dream of tutus and stage lights. To Uncle Don, thanks for the magic of other lights, airplanes and runways and getting lost in the enchanted maze of Carmel. And to my grandmother, Roxana Holmes Blanks: Grams, if I can always remember to approach life with even half of your grace, humor, and spunk, there'll be no hurdle I can't leap. I just want you to know, Grandpa's orchids will always bloom in my heart.

To Jerry's sisters, Sandra Lafferty and Nita Shoaf: thanks for making me welcome in your family. My special thanks to Viva Ellis, Jerry's mother. Viva, not only are you one of the most gracious and classy women I've ever met, you've also given me the greatest gift of my life: the opportunity to love your son.

Jerry Lynn Ellis, thanks for being You, thanks for being my partner, and thanks for making our love the greatest adventure in life. You and me, bud, forever and always. For that reason, I dedicate this book to you.

Bibliography

MacMahon, James A. *Deserts*. New York: Alfred A. Knopf (National Audubon Society Nature Guides), 1985.

McPhee, John. *Basin and Range*. New York: Farrar, Straus & Giroux,1980.

Stark, Peter. "As Freezing Persons Recollect the Snow, First Chill—then Stupor—Then the Letting Go." *Outside Magazine* (January 1997).

Thoreau, Henry David. *Walden*. New York: Penguin Books, 1986.

Debi Holmes-Binney is a freelance writer who has traveled extensively throughout the United States and abroad. When not traveling, she lives in Fort Payne, Alabama, on two hundred acres of unspoiled forest in the Southern Appalachian mountains. Her articles have appeared in *Amaryllis* and the *Salt Lake Tribune. Desert Sojourn* is her first book.

Selected Seal Titles

Canyon Solitude: A Woman's Solo River Journey Through Grand Canyon, by Patricia C. McCairen. $14.95, 1-58005-007-7. A remarkable solo expedition down one of the world's most spectacular rivers.

Solo: On Her Own Adventure, edited by Susan Fox Rogers. $12.95, 1-878067-74-5. Whether they light out for a day hike in the Adirondacks, bodyboard with dolphins off the California coast or pedal across New Zealand, each contributor to *Solo* describes the inspiring challenges and exhilarating rewards of going it alone.

All the Powerful Invisible Things: A Sportswoman's Notebook, by Gretchen Legler. $12.95, 1-878067-69-9. Filled with a deep respect for wilderness, this beautifully written memoir traverses Legler's decade-long journey of self-discovery and reveals the ineffable grace of an outdoor life.

The Curve of Time, by M. Wylie Blanchet. $14.95, 1-878067-27-3. The fascinating true adventure story of a woman who packed her five children into a twenty-five-foot boat and explored the coastal waters of the Pacific Northwest in the late 1920s.

Gifts of the Wild: A Woman's Book of Adventure, from the Editors of Adventura Books. $16.95, 1-58005-006-9. From the spectacular mountains of Patagonia to the mossy woods of the Pacific Northwest, *Gifts of the Wild* explores the transformative power of outdoor adventure in the lives of women.

Leading Out: Mountaineering Stories of Adventurous Women, edited by Rachel da Silva. $16.95, 1-58005-010-7. In more than twenty-five accounts by outstanding women climbers, this collection illustrates with eloquence and power how women are challenged and transformed by their experiences in the mountains.

Season of Adventure: Traveling Tales and Outdoor Journeys of Women Over 50, edited by Jean Gould. $15.95, 1-878067-81-8. Whether birdwatching in the Galápagos, camel-touring in Egypt or exploring the Pacific Cascades, these women display an uncommon *joie de vivre* and a keen awareness of their surroundings.

Femme d'Adventure: Travel Tales from Inner Montana to Outer Mongolia, by Jessica Maxwell. $14.00, 1-878067-98-2. Maxwell recounts tales of trailing humpback whales, braving whitewater rapids, catching a glimpse of tropical manatees, chasing wild mustangs and trotting the globe from Ireland to Venice and beyond.

SEAL PRESS publishes many books of fiction and nonfiction by women writers. If you are unable to obtain a Seal Press title from a bookstore or would like a free catalog of our books, please order from us directly by calling 800-754-0271. Visit our website at www.sealpress.com.